MEXICO

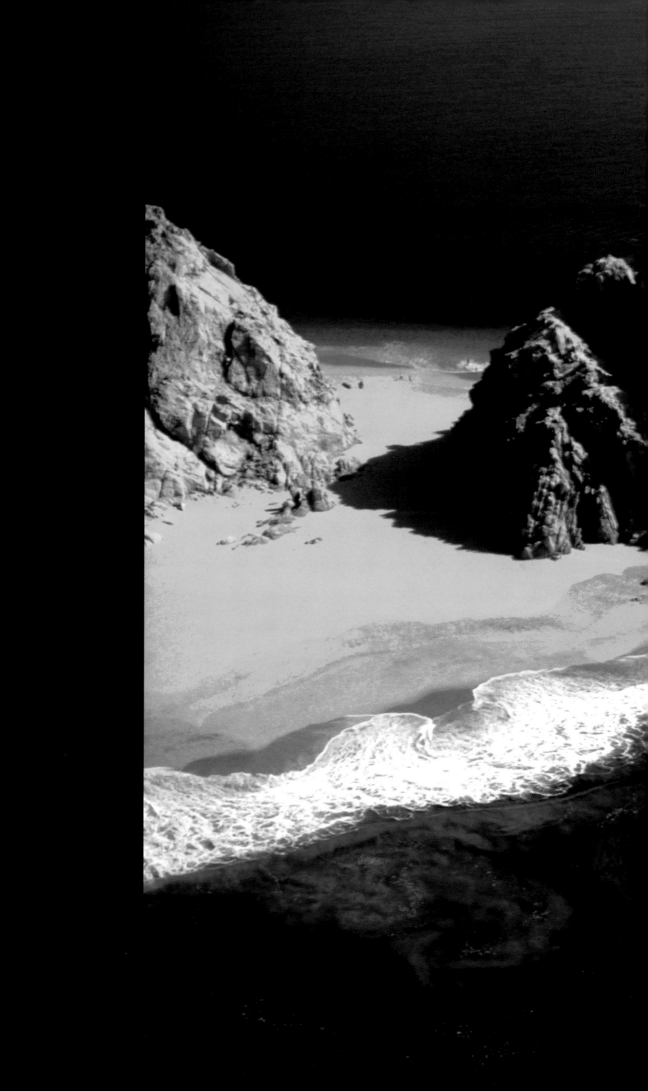

HOUSES OF LOS CABOS

HOUSES OF LOS CABOS

Project Editor

MAURICIO MARTÍNEZ

Photography

RIGOBERTO MORENO

Text

ALICIA ALDRETE

AMAROMA EDICIONES

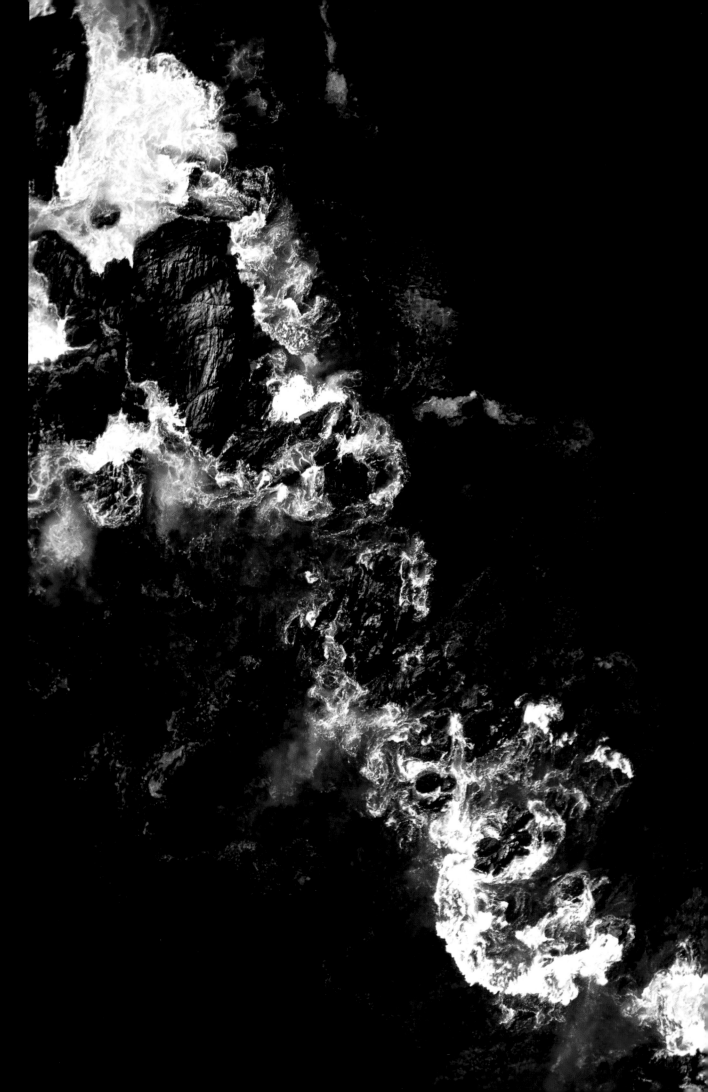

HOUSES OF LOS CABOS

PROJECT EDITOR
Mauricio Martínez

PHOTOGRAPHY
Rigoberto Moreno
Photos at page 20 and at the bottom of 98:
Nancy Aldrete

TEXT
Alicia Aldrete

RESEARCH
Alicia Aldrete
Francisco Javier Ibarra

ILLUSTRATION
Josel

EDITORIAL COUNSELLOR
Rocío Guillén

TRANSLATION
Lucinda A. Mayo
Stephen Gilbert
Debra Nagao

SUPERVISED EDITORS
Augusta Cobar
Ángeles Fahara
Miriam Reyes

STYLE CORRECTION
Marcelino Becerril Aguirre
Jesús de Loza Paiz

TYPOGRAPHY
Ángeles Fahara

PRE-PRESS
Groppe

DESIGN AND
EXECUTIVE PRODUCTION
Amaroma Ediciones

AMAROMA EDICIONES
Av. Vallarta 1835-2, Col. Americana, C.P. 44140
Guadalajara, Jalisco, México
Tel. 3 616-5343. Fax 3 616-5346
E-mail: amaroma@vinet.com.mx

English version: ISBN 970 92410 1 X
Spanish version: ISBN 970 92410 0 1

PRINTED IN HONG KONG
BY GLOBAL INTERPRINT, INC.

PRESENTATION
Raúl Aceves

PROLOGUE
Mauricio Martínez

LOS CABOS, UNEXPECTED LANDSCAPE
Francisco Javier Ibarra

CASAS DE LOS CABOS
Alicia Aldrete

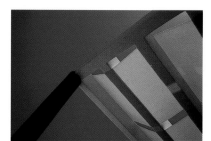

*T*his book tells one story: the desire to build the perfect paradisal refuge, at the edge of the known world. Architectonic nests where modernity is dressed in luxury and comfort, where fortunate and adventurous hermits might take their ease in rustic splendour on the solitary coast of Baja California, next to the play of the limpid blues of sea and sky.

In contrast to those pilgrims who seek a spiritual «world's end» somewhere beyond the Milky Way, these travellers, arrived from many parts of the world, have found another resting place: a natural, interior sanctuary where – like the whales – they can step outside of life's business for a moment, and take a little of life's elixir, before returning to the fray.

Few, indeed, chose to disappear into the desert, but all have sworn to realize a dream, to leave an aesthetic trace on the landscape of their desire. These traces, translated into words and photographic images constitute the archetectonics of this book; houses to be inhabited by the imagination. To enter the book is to disembark onto a virgin beach, full of surprise, or to posess the key to new worlds, windows of intimate generosity. The photographers, writers, and the architects who were interviewed for this project have shared their visions and testimonies and offer us a closer look, an interior shot of recovered history, of a constructed landscape in all its magnificence.

Houses of Los Cabos reveals the qualities of a little known part of Mexico, where architecture is integrated perfectly into the surrounding natural landscape, to generate a tourist area of unsurpassed beauty and incomparable serenity. With this book, Amaroma has won for itself a place of honor in Mexican publishing, and confirmed its reputation as a designer and publisher of fine books. I look forward to more pleasant surprises like this one, an authentic voyage into aesthetic experience.

Raúl Aceves

Some travellers discover lost valleys,
turquoise blue in the salt desert,
whiteness that journeys across the sky.
Some travellers stay and live
beside the blue, in their rocky nests
like disciples of the eagles.

Some men become eagles
as some eagles become men.
Others become salt in the sea
and carry the legend away on the tides.

Raúl Aceves

*L*os Cabos seems one of those places where the future begins. In one of the oldest regions of human habitat in Mexico, as shown by the caves and wall paintings of the San Francisco Sierra, has come an urban development announcing the new century.

In the manner of a magnetic center at the end of an almost insular territory, where the Pacific Ocean and the Sea of Cortés come together, somewhat remove from the cultural dynamic of central Mexico, and within reach of the influences of other continents, Los Cabos in Baja California, like part of an unsuspected Mexican treasure, is undergoing a marvelous and vigorous transformation.

The houses of Los Cabos are recent phenomena in Mexican architecture, buildings which co-exist in harmony at some times, and in contrast at others; they dialogue among each other in their own eclectic manner, speaking of different cultural influences, formal values and life styles.

Only people disposed to challenge, with a taste for adventure, with the ability to dream and to make dreaming real, can live in places like this.

Architects, contractors and homeowners belong to this category. Together they have undertaken the labors of raising impressive buildings which appear more the materialization of inspiration than mere accomodation to climate, technology, or cultures. The results are surprising in the diversity of forms, spaces and materials. Concepts are as individual as the inhabitants and builders, and each house is its own paradigm.

Houses of Los Cabos has tried to capture this period of Mexican architecture in the sensitive narrative of Alicia Aldrete, the remarkable photographic focus of Rogoberto Moreno, and the historical vision of Francisco Javier Ibarra.

The adventure begins as you turn the page....

Mauricio Martínez

Los Cabos, unexpected landscape

A journey that never ends

Francisco Javier Ibarra

Naming a locale can truly affect its destiny. The first reference to the word «California» was in the medieval epic poem *Song of Roland*, written in France at the beginning of the eleventh century. In this work, considered one of the pillars of French literature, a marvelous North African land, exclusively inhabited by women, appeared. Called «*Califerne*», and located by the anonymous author in the Berber region, this fortified city or *kalas* (which provides the root of the word California), was home to the queens and princesses of the mythical tribe of *Ben-Ifren*, sometimes called *Kalas-Ifren*.

Four centuries later, after his discovery of America, Christopher Columbus decided to give his imagination free rein and, in a detailed chronicle of his first voyage to the «Indies» he referred for the first time — without giving a name or directions for getting there — to a fantastic island in the West, occupied solely by women armed with bows and arrows, who occasionally visited men for amorous pursuits. Five years later, Columbus mentioned in another account of his journeys that he had navigated toward this earthly paradise in the west.

Although the Genovese admiral didn't, even in his fevered imagination, link the fabled isle of the Amazons either geographically or politically with this alleged Eden, other navigators and writers would take it upon themselves to join the two, then seek to locate this invented territory.

A writer of books on chivalry, and councilman of the Spanish town of Medina del Campo, at the start of the sixteenth century sought to interrelat the *Song of Roland*'s city of females with Columbus' prodigious fables. This novelist, Garcí Ordoñez de Montalvo, wrote a successful, popular and timely story of knights-in-armor titled *Las sergas de Esplandían (The Exploits of Esplandían)*. The fifth volume in the famous saga of Amadis of Gaul, the book was initially published in 1510 and widely read throughout the sixteenth and seventeenth centuries, particularly in Spain, Portugal, England, France and Germany. *The Exploits of Esplandían* gave literary merit, and even more tantalizing legendary status, to the myth of California:

«Be it known that at the right-hand side of the Indies there was an island known as California, a veritable earthly paradise, where dwelt a settlement of black women, and no men; their manner of living was quite Amazonian. These women, true warriors who used to adorn themselves with pearls and gold, loyally served their queen Calafia. Their weaponry was of gold, as was the equipage of the animals which they tamed and rode: there was no other metal in the land. On this isle of the fiercest rocky cliffs ever seen, grew the most fragrant roses in the world. This place called California was also home to many griffons, chimeras, dragons and other marvels.»

Twenty-three years after the first edition of *The Exploits of Esplandían*, a Spanish adventurer whose eyes had never tired of reading these fables actually killed a fellow-voyager, a man named Becerra, in order to claim the questionable glory of having been first to set foot on Baja California's soil. Fortún Jiménez' self-satisfaction and delight in what he saw there did not last long, as he was killed by the region's indigenous tribe. Thus, Fortún was not terribly fortunate: nor were many other would-be conquerors who failed to tame the peninsula's savage beauty.

Since then, the mythologizing of this land has become part of its destiny. For over two centuries it was considered to be an island (if not a paradise of invincible women), in spite of clear indications to adventurers, mapmakers, missionaries and simple travelers that it was a peninsular appendage to the territory of New Spain.

Over many years it was also believed that warrior women did exist here, attracting men with their charms like gorgeous sirens, making love with them before murdering them on the beaches or in the vast loneliness of the deserts. When pregnancy resulted, acording to legend, the enchantress was implacable: if the child were a boy he was mercilessly killed; if a girl, she was allowed to thrive and enter the exclusively female community.

Another legend that is still heard throughout the southern peninsula assures us that any person who eats fruits or blossoms from the island of «Mogote», will never leave the region alive nor live to see their place of origin, but will be condemned to spend the rest of their days in the strange and mysterious paradise of Baja California.

Nowadays, myths, legends and enchantments persist in Baja California, despite the winds and tides of economic development that bring with them less magical currents, such as the social problems and inequities that are the other face of modernity and progress. Occult fictions have been buried away like a mirror we won't peer into for fear of learning that our would be «ultra-modern» image has been disfigured by accelerated growth over the past 30 years. But the past rushes in, one way or another, and continues to feed Baja California's vitality even today. Though it daily grows as one of the most visited areas, peopled almost to the saturation point, yet «Baja California always seems an unknown land, and each person who arrives here becomes a discoverer. Who can argue with the thought that each rediscovery is the first ever?» (Fernándo Jordán, in *El otro México*, or *The Other Mexico*.)

Waters that embrace fire

Between the luminous and eternally blue sky («eternal» except in rainy season, when huge dark clouds appear!), and the buffeting waters of the Pacific Ocean and Sea of Cortés, Baja California extends along the northern part of Mexico like a land full of promises. Here one can grasp everything beautiful, solve every enigma, immerse oneself in the mysteries of nature, feel the savage splendor of diverse landscapes, delve into a fascinating mix of history and culture, spend unforgettable leisure, encounter chances for development, and make dreams come alive.

Baja California Sur's origins go back to the Cenozoic Era, more than 100 million years ago, when the peninsula began to separate from the rest of what is now Mexican territory. Then it acquired its own geographical features, from a series of powerful seismic shifts and the sinking of the surface of the region that now comprises Sonora and Sinaloa. In fact, this peninsula is part of the Pacific plate geological system, and of the phenomenon known as the San Andreas fault: the northern part of the Gulf of California coincides with the southern indentations of the Elsinore and San Jacinto faults.

After the violent creation of the Bermejo (Vermilion) Sea or Gulf of California — which from the seventeenth century onwards would be known as the Sea of Cortés — the rise of rough mountain ridges, volcanoes, streams winding through canyons, varied vegetation, and desert plains that extend from Guerrero Negro to Cabo San Lucas, were all configured. Today, they determine the landscape and climate that makes up today's life in Baja California Sur: everpresent heat, barely whetted by summer rains and the tropical storms that may unexpectedly become hurricanes; infinite deserts full of cactus, mountain chains reaching dizzyingly to the sea by way of steep cliffs and impinging bays, plains populated by wind-tossed tumbleweeds, as well as mezquite,

saguaro, nopal and many other cactus varieties. Here also, islands that may not be the legendary hideaways of sirens, but may yet be described as paradises; seas where whales frolic and dolphins leap, while fishermen catch quantities of abalone, clams, tuna, swordfish, shrimp, marlin, sailfish, lobster and manta ray.

Because of the often paradoxical beauty of her flora and fauna, it's still not uncommon for travelers — mesmerized, misled, dreaming or simply bewitched — to confuse Baja California Sur with a legendary land of marvels. Like the «raft made of stone» that José Saramago calls his homeland of Portugal, this land has freed itself of the continental mass, to float in the Pacific. On the «raft» of Baja California Sur, one can become a dazzled Alice, going through the Looking Glass to the Other Side of the Moon, to a place where dreams can be seen, touched and relived.

In days of old, the native plants led this to be called the «Perfumed Land»; today both flora and fauna provide magic touches of loveliness. At the same time the area battles to save some endangered species, there proliferates an overwhelming range of colors and forms, many found only in this region. The peninsula's natural convergence of plant and animal varieties has been studied since the times of Spanish conquest, from early chroniclers such as

the priest Miguel del Barco (1706-1790) in his *Natural History and Critique of Old California*, to such contemporary researchers as Aureliano de Vivanco (*Baja California Day-by-Day*), Ray Cannon (*The Sea of Cortés*), and Ann Zwinger (*A Desert Country Near the Sea: A Natural History of the Cape Region of Baja California*.)

Here vegetation's «candles» burn in every desert cranny; cactus limbs twist and writhe as if exorcising demons, their thorn fingers scratching the sky; resins once used as incense release their sacred scents into air freshened by date-palms. Purple and yellow flowers restore life to mountains that remain barren much of the year, lush *copa de oro* and *damiana* blooms adding heady perfume to the fields. Rattlesnakes ask no permission as they glide ominously; giant hares are a hallucinatory sight on highways and golf courses; from their breezy watchtowers vultures track coyotes and foxes. Roadrunners pass as if pursued by demons; pelicans hover level with the sea at all hours, and throughout the day seals wait for someone to toss a ball. Sharks sharpen their teeth in the aquatic depths; sea elephants challenge one another for dominance; whales return year after year that we may listen to their promises and rites of love for those near and far.

For anyone arriving in Baja California Sur by air, land or sea, the region jumps into view in all its violent contrasts and unsuspected complicities. Deserts that produce a range of ochres, yellows and browns all year, but at the first sign of rain create a panoply of greens — and greens more beautiful than anywhere else, because they are so momentary. Mountain chains, where the grays of this semi-arid climate's spiny plants create a captivating palette with the indigos and violets whose birthplace is the hills and mountain peaks.

Also, jagged and unyielding coasts, whose sands spread out in gentle gold; where the water's constantly changing palette splashes upon the peninsula — turquoise green at the shore dissolving into cobalt blue, deep azure blending with the silver tones far out in the ocean. And the light touch of terracottas and reds along the horizon line, with that peculiar coppery shimmer that reminds us that the Sea of Cortés was once named Bermejo, or Vermilion, for the abundance of microscopic plants and plankton that colored it.

Bathed by the waters of the Pacific and the Gulf of California, the peninsula is a warm and sinuous rock forming itself into valleys, plains, deserts and mountains. Baja California Sur is a grand «No Exit», a marvelous crossroads, a land of fire trapped between two immense waters that embrace it, refresh it, move it to and fro, recreate it into something alive with amazing perplexity.

Mirrors in the Desert

Footprints of the first humans to walk upon what is now Baja California Sur date from 10,000 B.C. Marks of seashells, bones, skulls, hunting and fishing nets and spears, palmleaf baskets, ochre-colored ornaments fashioned of seeds and beads, among other material culture, signify that two primitive cultural groups flourished here. In the central zone, the population has been called the «Palm Culture»; in the north, the «Comondú».

Perhaps the most meaningful cultural and artistic inheritance from these communities is a series of cave paintings, as mysterious as they are savagely beautiful, which were created around 3000 B.C. We can now study these in various caves, rocky crags and crannies amidst the Guadalupe, San Francisco, San Borja and San Juan mountains, and even in the vicinities of Cabo San Lucas and San José del Cabo.

These paintings, whose enigmatic origins have yet to be fully revealed, portray — in black, red and ochre tones — giant human figures, playful deer, serpents that stretch across the rock face, turtles with the spiral forms that typically represent time's cycles; rabbits that jump innocently here and there, fish swimming in air, fabulous animals, and birds about to confidently launch themselves into the sky.

Towards the middle of the sixteenth century, when the first Spanish expeditions arrived, Baja California Sur was inhabited by tribes descended from the Palm and Comondú

peoples. These tribes, the Cochimíes, Guaycuras and Pericúes, each had their own language and cultural patterns. It's believed that these groups reached the peninsula from North America, having originated in Asia. There also exists a theory, particularly concerning the Pericúes because of their morphology and diverse cultural vestiges that cannot be linked to the other two groups, that they arrived here suddenly from across the southern Pacific and one of the islands of Oceania. This hypothesis, remains open to further scientific confirmation.

Seduced by the legends of an island dominated by women who lived amidst gold and pearls, Spanish conquerors made various expeditions to Baja California Sur. Following Fortún Jiménez' initial discovery, in 1535 Hernan Cortés made his own landing, in what is now La Paz. Cortés christened the area «the Port and Bay of Santa Cruz (Holy Cross)»; he didn't conquer the peninsula, but returned to Mexico City in 1537 and later sent several emissaries to attempt to overcome this lawless land. The last of those he sent, Francisco de Ulloa, was lost along with his ship «Trinidad» in the depths of the Pacific. According to those who still live on Mal Arrimo (Bad Landfall) Bay, at full moon one can still hear the waves clearly repeating, «Ulloa, Ulloa...»

Years passed and various expeditionary forces made their own attempts to conquer and colonize. Terrible battles between natives and invaders occurred, up and down the peninsula, until little by little the Europeans began to impose their law of superior force, weapons and technological knowledge. But Spanish conquest also involved the spiritual sphere, and actually the domination of Baja California can be attributed to Jesuit and Franciscan missionaries

who came here. The Jesuits remained in Baja California Sur from 1683 when Father Eusebio Francisco Kino founded his first mission in La Paz, until the order was expelled from New Spain in 1768.

The Jesuits' tireless labor in building missions throughout Baja California Sur was continued by the Franciscans, led by Friar Junipero Serra. The architectural style of both Jesuit and Franciscan missions, along with ancient indigenous forms, have influenced subsequent construction, and the representative local style still appears in both public and private Baja California buildings.

Sparsely populated, and isolated from the rest of Mexico, Baja California watched from afar as the end of the Viceregal period became the fight for Independence, followed by the national rifts provoked by the Reform Laws. Baja California was virtually ensconced in its own struggles, borne of the deterioration and abandonment of the early missions. There were attacks by various pirate bands, the loss and larceny of treasures from the Manila Galleon while in Baja California waters, extravagant acts as well as misunderstandings — including one with Chilean sailors just as Mexican Independence was proclaimed in San José del Cabo; along with the collective heroic defense of the peninsula's riches and natural resources against the greed of England, France, the U.S. and Japan; and of Mexican sovereignty, when their land was invaded by the U.S. in 1847. At the same time, the fishing, mining and salt extraction industries were slowly developing.

In 1888 the peninsula was divided into two districts, and La Paz became the capital of Baja California Sur. Although the constitutional designation of the districts made for somewhat greater commercial and industrial contact with the rest of Mexico, Baja California Sur in particular remained isolated, introverted and lightly populated during the regime of Porfirio Díaz (ruefully remembered locally for a phrase from one of his official speeches, which ended, «Poor Baja California!»), through the revolutionary era, and throughout a good part of the period that saw much of Mexico's political, economic, social and cultural modernization.

On February 7, 1931, the district of Baja California Sur became a federal territory and, after a forty-three years wait, succeeded to free and sovereign statehood on October 3, 1974. Full integration of Baja California Sur with the rest of the country and the world meant that ports were opened, and its enormous economic and touristic potential could be realized.

During the 1950's Baja California Sur's beautiful beaches, mesmerizing deserts and historic missions began to attract national and international tourists; however, it was not until the decade of the 1970's that the construction of the transpeninsular highway, the Loreto and San José del Cabo airports, and quality hotels and resorts encouraged creation of the Los Cabos-San José del Cabo, and Loreto-Nepoló tourist corridors. Three areas of tourist development: from Guerrero Negro to Ciudad Constitucion, La Paz to Todos los Santos, and Los Barriles to Cabo San Lucas, added to the attractions the region provides.

As Fernando Jordán writes, in a book that captures the very essence of old California,

«Baja California was, and is now, rich or poor, beautiful or gruesome, inaccessible or hospitable — depending on the lens through which you view it.» From such a perspective,

the Baja California peninsula has throughout history been a desert full of mirrors that reflect the will of its visitors; their ambitions, intentions and spirit. Now that Baja California has opened itself to progress, the tradition continues. The mirrors just multiply the images and dreams traced in the desert sands, of those who taste the juicy and aphrodisiac fruits and find themselves unable to leave this enchanting place.

One of the first, most intense sensations a new visitor to Los Cabos receives, not only from the landscape and geography but from the words and deeds of people from San José to San Lucas, is a feeling of being not only on an island, but at the very end of the world.

There seems to be nothing beyond what is right here; when one reaches the farthest western point of Baja California Sur, one is at the very beginning, or the end, of the habitable world. It is indeed a kind of *Finisterre* or Land's End, such as that mentioned in the accounts of Roman, Celtic, Portuguese and finally Spanish sailors.

This sense is literally felt in Cabo Falso: while some romantically insist that the majestic natural sculpture of El Arco, where the Sea of Cortés and Pacific come together, is the true Land's End, the truth is that here there's nothing

more than the boundless presence of the largest ocean on the planet.

Through this lens, this spirit that covers the region, Los Cabos is an isolated land, which at the same time reveals all its history, its openness to the possibilities of the human universe. Where the murmur of the sea hits the sand of the shore, waves come and go in a rhythm that invites contemplation; inviting also a mood of fleeting time. The protective sky extends over the golden ochre tones of the desert with its spiny plants, some huge, some diminutive; the turquoise, emerald, silver and russet tides highlight the wildly impressive size of the the Pacific and the Sea of Cortés where they join. And there, just where the border between sea and sand dissolves, Los Cabos is a beacon lighting our way, our vision and intuition, through known and unknown — into magnificent beauty.

Far from presenting this land as a bucolic Arcadia, the actual facts of Los Cabos' life paint a more interesting history: the fierceness of the legendary Pericúes against evangelist-conquerors, assaults by British and Dutch pirates upon the Manila Galleon, victorious battles fought by residents of Los Cabos and San José against U.S. invaders. Then, the commercial rise of San José del Cabo as the twentieth century began, the

fishing industry in Cabo San Lucas, efforts to withstand the fury of cyclones, the growth of tourism and the construction that seems never-ending throughout the municipality; and the problems of urban infrastructure that have come with the rapid population growth of the past twenty years.

Accustomed to solving conflicts no matter how serious, Los Cabos still wears its seductive veil, exerts its magnetism, and stands as one of the most gorgeous places in Mexico or the world. With its own rhythm, neither rushing nor pausing in its pace, the region rises to its latest challenges.

It is enough to tour Cabo San Lucas, San José del Cabo, and the 33 km. that link (and on occasion divide) them —dream-laden beaches where life finds its own sensual, joyous, lighthearted dimensions; water that captivates and dazzles the eye; centers of tourist development that have offered innumerable sources of work; the zone's consolidation, its postmodern fate at the crossroads; many and various cultural influences allowing infinite expressive potencial; diverse building projects, public and private, intimate and simultaneously cosmopolitan.

Visit El Arco and spend the morning on Playa del Amor (Beach of Love, which took its name, say certain chroniclers, because a «fancy» lady, Doña Chepa, received her distinguished fishermen clients here), play golf by the shore or discover the towering cascades of sand that rise over the Sea of Cortés' waters, motorcycle to old Cabo Falso and walk its dunes, explore the Pedregal's cliffs and crags, wander the forest of metaphors growing among the *cardo* and *cholla* cactus. If you take a dip in the wide Pacific, if you spend a night of revelry that ends or begins in the human tangle of «Squid Roe», if you bask on Santa Maria beach's sun and descend the rocks to brave the waves, or fly in an «ultralight» admiring the infinite beauty from San José or San Lucas, if you enjoy a drink of *damiana* while lingering before El Arco, you'll find that you've still not exhausted all the reasons for falling in love with Los Cabos.

However, there is one very compelling reason for leaving your spirit and substance here and it is provided by the best houses of Los Cabos: simple and elegant, fantastic and tactile, intuitive and calculated, liberated and unexpected. Original and architecturally purposeful, daring and proud, the Houses of Los Cabos are built where the land ends, the sky and sea are eternally open to portent, and paradise is a reality.

Dwellings at Land's End

The appearance of new public and private structures is an important sign of Baja California Sur's growth wave over the past decades. Expecially in the state's southern zone, these lend an air of sophistication, durability, architectural function and beauty to the peninsula's nights and days.

Even beyond their distinctive design, their compositions and solutions for meeting the landscape's aesthetic, their plays of light and shadow, their brilliant style; Los Cabos' best houses give us an opportunity to observe forms created for their inhabitants' enjoyment. This visual tour is another, perhaps more passionate way of knowing the nature of this unfettered land, of understanding and delighting in the seas of dreams, prodigious deserts, underwater abysses, infinitely blue sky: this Eden devised and hailed in antiquity, now within our reach; this marvel that is Los Cabos.

The dwellings at Land's End that are presented in this book don't belong to a particular architectural style or fashion, nor have they any creative paradigm but the imaginative freedom shared by owners with the architects who have translated their tastes, affinities and passions into splendid shelter.

These homes can be grouped, for practical purposes, into those of the Palmilla residential community, those located near the San José del Cabo-Cabo San Lucas touristic corridor, and those built in the area known as the Pedregal. Or, they may be thought of as houses facing either the Pacific or the Sea of Cortés.

More important, is the book's purpose of allowing each home to reveal itself, in all its spirit and architectural truth, to the reader. Its essence as a dwelling, its details and passages, its connection to the region's landscape, its formal risks, large and small ideas and solutions, interior and exterior design, its gardens, its way of handling movement and light, its protection of inhabitants' privacy, its chromatic balance, inspirations and evocations, infinity trapped in a swimming pool or stone carpet original, use of materials; the definition of dwelling space for human life between deserts of water and sand, the vitality and serenity of Los Cabos.

To contemplate the castles at Land's End, the houses of Los Cabos, is visually to enter the timeless conviction of the wind, water, fire, earth; of the region's residents, voyagers, explorers, adventurers and curiosity seekers; of the sea and desert as they whisper to one another: «In Los Cabos the journey never ends...»

CASA ALEGRÍA

EMOTION MADE VISIBLE, DESIGNED WITH FEELING

BYRL BINKLEY, ARCHITECT
PLAN AND CONSTRUCTION

ROLAND SCHULZ, ARCHITECT
ORIGINAL CONCEPT

Very white, very contemporary, it stands, as we'd expect in Los Cabos, atop a cliff; sharing neither terrain nor vista with the rest of the world. The house is inner-directed, oriented toward the heart of a family that has decided to make its home here.

Of German origin, the owners' traditionally orderly culture is expressed in every meticulously-detailed inch of the house. They've kept records of each wall as it was built, each stone that was incorporated into the property's layout.

Rising from a circular base, it assumes various interior levels. It combines comfort, functionality and beauty –remarkable beauty.

A fairly understated main door opens into the house, and a gate allows scant sight-lines to the interior. Several large stones relieve the symmetry of the walls, and flowers bedeck the wall facing the sun-baked street; other colorful elements invite closer inspection.

Warm Welcome

When the doorbell is rung the owner, a man very Nordic in appearance, comes out to greet the visitor. He is warm, kind, low-key and dignified, perfectly matched with this house.

A narrow open-air passage leads to a double-door entrance. Walls are strongly vertical, but softened by rooflines which echo the horizon's natural curve

The white of the walls underscores the contrast of the house's jubilant presence with its dramatic landscape.

While the entrance's gray stone is neutral, touches of pink on the first riser of the steps keeps the eye from complacency.

Some terms that may be used to define the style of Casa Alegría are contemporary, casual and precise. The architect and owners agreed upon all the utility, beauty, and privacy the spaces required, from the time these were mere sketches on paper. Colors, textures, and materials figured in their conversations; there were exhaustive exchanges over the placement of a rock, the curvature of the terrace, the location of the jacuzzi; the result is a decided sense of each element rightly, unequivocally belonging just where it is.

The vestibule is matter-of-fact in its simplicity. It opens onto a circular hall upon which other circular spaces converge: the kitchen, dining room, family room and stairwell. Everything is splendidly white, yet exults in warmth and good taste.

This house is emotion made visible. When it was completed, the owners published their thanks in the local newspaper, to all who took part in the project, from the architect to the humblest laborer, with full names and words of acknowledgment. Their house reflects their humanity and love for the community.

The kitchen at the house's center is crowned by a handsomely-fitted cupola. A double bar topped in green-toned ceramic tile picks up the patina of the adjacent chairs.

Lighting has been designed to accentuate the home's methodically-planned interiors. At one end of the house, the living room has a fireplace with a display of animal horns over it, flanked by built-in shelves. A collection of alphabetized CD's reflect the orderliness encountered throughout the house. In the elevated dining room at the other end, recessed display cases hold carefully chosen family pieces.

The leather of the living room furniture, in a green tone edging into gray, again appears in the wood surfaces of the dining room.

The room's windowpanes echo in the round glass-topped table, and the space is punctuated by a spare assortment of beloved objects.

At the front entrance, the view explodes between two pillars, one pink, the other purple, against the house's ever-present, immaculate white. The terrace adjoins the hall, but is distinguished as an exterior space by rustic leather chairs placed between it and the expanse of the hallway. Between the pillars and a perilous precipice, a low undulating wall is silhouetted: the beach stretches out below, caressed by the sea which draws the eye to the horizon.

Forceful on the outside, inside the home reflects supreme care and orderly detail. The result is a structure that responds to the countryside around, and turns inward to reveal a wealth of forms and sense impressions.

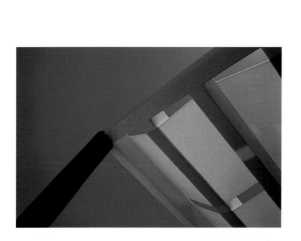

Vertices and curves exist side-by-side in white harmony. Plants and flowers are located as precisely as the carefully-selected stones which here and there declare their permanence. As a whole, the building addresses the ambiguities between extreme linearity and the sensuality of curves. Each facade, corner, every inch displays dynamically contrasting forms. Even window dimensions suggest that they've been hung within striking rectangles that accommodate themselves to the concave wall, and *vice versa*.

Constant attention to the home's comfort quotient appears in dozens of details, such as the small tube inserted in a flowerbox overlooking the cliff, which we learn is there to hold a patio umbrella in the afternoons.

The home's circularity is repeated in several spaces, subtly, as if walls, terraces, were embracing select pieces of furniture and design features. This play of rounded surfaces may be seen in the master bedroom, guestroom, and study.

Vertical force is also prominently employed in large windows and shelves. The resulting harmony between rectilinear and curvilinear is evident throughout.

Privacy a Priority

When the owner bought the property and scanned the horizon, his gaze fell on the most proximate house, which stood at some remove. He immediately introduced himself to those neighbors and assured them that none of his windows, terraces or entryways would affect their privacy. Wishing to guarantee privacy for both properties, he followed through on his promise in several ways.

Casa Alegría stands on a high elevation; it faces no other construction, and the privacy so precious to its dwellers is extended to other Los Cabos residents. The house doesn't «look back», neither to the past nor to the surrounding countryside: its view, from any location, takes in the sea, the cliffs, the beach, and the sky.

The circular guest area is a separate, and very private, unit. Its upper level is occupied by a kitchenette and a sitting room. This is owner's favorite spot, because «...it invites me to think, to read, to reflect, without any company other than the view framed by the landscape.» Such serenity is not unusual in any room here, but this sitting room is especially welcoming.

In the beginning, the kitchenette served more often as an open-air terrace. However, the winds from the sea changed the owners' plans and they decided to strike a «non-aggression pact»

Every corner of the building is in harmony with nature, respecting what was already there. It is present without imposing, offering itself to the light each afternoon.

with the weather by building an organically-shaped wall and installing rectangular windows.

The guest bedrooms are located right below and are identical, each with the same comfort, privacy and appreciation for the landscape.

This architectural arrangement allows guests and family to be as communal or solitary as they'd like.

Reincarnation

The house is alive with sensations and feelings, yet each of its spaces is imbued with order and functionality.

The kitchen hides a small studio where everything the woman of the house needs is within reach. There she can be seen catching up on correspondence, or selecting photographs for filling an album. Next to the entrance hall there is an office where the man of the house deals with matters needing his attention. In the

garage there is a workshop for repairs that range from fixing a picture frame to changing parts on the jet ski, the mountain bike, or the water pump. All the equipment has its place; sports gear, vehicles, and household replacement parts.

Next door is the machine room, situated affably beside an enormous rock «that was already here when we arrived». The room was arranged around the boulder, and pipes and electrical connections have been left exposed to make maintenance here easier.

«It's everything I dreamed of,» she comments, «...and more.»

And indeed, the pleasure that the property evokes for its owners shows, in the care they lavish upon everyday homemaking, and the generosity with which the house responds. The warmth between inhabitants and house is two-way: they radiate warmth, and the home surrounds them with its own degree of care.

The storage room contains the photographic history of the family bound in leather and divided into several volumes. It is a faithful record of trips throughout the Bay region before coming to live in Los Cabos, of many episodes in their lives, and of the process of building the house.

«I was Mexican in another life, but with the passage of time I forgot the language,» he says, in German-accented English and with a Latin smile. His wife, devoted to him, shares all his passions.

From such devotion and passion, they've made a home which bespeaks gratitude and balance. Their environment is an ode to design elements in symbiosis with human endeavor.

The individual responsible for converting these elements into a house was the architect Byrl Birkley. He specializes in eliciting his clients' wishes, and translates what they tell him into the distinctive arrangement of walls surmounted by a roof which becomes their home; Both activities he shares with his wife, Lucy, partly so that their daughter, Lysette, may appreciate the formal lessons his profession provides.

The building process was intense, especially for anyone unfamiliar with Mexican techniques for laying foundations, building and plastering walls, and pouring concrete for roofing. There were difficult months, during which the owners and Byrl anxiously followed developments.

Casa Bashforth

Barely contained sensuality

Próspero Tapia, Architect
Plan and construction

This home is a work of fine detail, almost in filigree. It is set on a cliff, crafted with the same meticulous care as a piece of jewelry. Magic is crammed into less than 400 square meters of construction on an irregular piece of land measuring 1,500 meters.

Casa Bashforth has a split personality: shy to expose itself, but eloquent at the right moment. It won't allow itself to be taken in at a glance. It is a proper young lady of the nineteenth century: prim and proper on the outside, burning and passionate on the inside. She gives itself only to whom she chooses.

«The architecture transforms the cry of sensuality of the surroundings into a murmur, which filters through the walls of the house.» In Casa Bashforth, that murmur becomes louder and there is no way to contain it; each object inspires its own «flight to freedom».

Open Manipulation

«The original intention was to give the house an Eden-like atmosphere, a space allowing full enjoyment of the surroundings in the midst of complete privacy,» comments Próspero Tapia, the architect responsible for the plan of Casa Bashforth.

The public face of the house, the one that can be seen from the side with the steep street, reveals little. It seems to be merely an austere facade. Ornamental plants are added to this apparently humble abode, as visual obstacles concealing what is hidden inside.

This house has what all houses should have, declares Tapia. «A very conservative appearance on the outside» a modest face that shows no desire to share what is within with others. Inside, a long vestibule is the first thing that meets the eye, but without letting us know anything special awaits us. Because of its design, the vestibule forces the visitor to walk quickly, to find out what lies inside, at the back, which is really just the beginning of a house that perches on the mountainside, ready to break away over the rocks, and that gazes out brazenly at an endless sea, melting into the sky.

Without warning, the atmosphere changes and sensuality captures one's spirit. The spacious view contains sensual dunes, while a Gaudí-style vault that seems to sway back and forth in different directions, covers the living room. The arch points, in seeming jest, in several different directions at the same time in an extravagant display of form and power.

Casa Bashforth sprawls over the mountain top, in a daring play of architecture and nature. It is conceived of as an element. To seize the immensity of the surroundings, a frank attempt to bring the deep sea to a manageable scale.

For Próspero Tapia, «It is a way of imitating the nature that surrounds us.» It is a frank attempt to emulate the sway of the palm trees caressed by the ocean breeze, mounds of sand blocking out the comings and goings of the wind, and skies which appear to be undecided about their hues.

There is magic, manipulation with the best intentions. People are victims of well-being without even realizing it. They are puppets of subtle, absorbing pleasure, emanating from the spaces around. It is a language that appeals to unconscious levels of understanding.

The environment created by means of forms, objects, and materials defines each area in Casa Bashforth. Utility is evident by the way that space is filled without any attempt at apology. Everything is presented with the simplicity that comes from good planning, without risking beauty at the cost of usefulness.

Even the roofs play a role in Tapia's project. You don't really know if you are above or below some other part of the house. Finally on the outside, the roofs work together to fit into the landscape. The tiles covering the roof are not an obstacle, rather they are decorative, to be appreciated from the point of view of several windows.

The rocks of the mountain cascade toward the terrace. The ocean does not interrupt the pleasures of the interior, but calmly stretches out, very much at home, from the master bedroom, the swimming pool, the jacuzzi. The pillars of strong, volcanic stone and solid form frame the immensity of the surrounding elements and bring them within reach.

Fistfuls of Stars

Beneath the dynamic, organic roof, the living room and dining room create a workmanlike atmosphere. Both display simple furnishings, with a profusion of well-carved wood contributing to the sensuality of the house, including to vanes of the fans, ending in sharply edged, curved contours, while Indian stone cut into whimsical forms covers the floor.

The entire construction is composed of areas that are at once vast, yet of human scale. At play are the contrasts between the human and the immensity of the countryside, the blend of sea and sky. This is the way Próspero Tapia takes the measure of external beauty and frames it with architecture.

One example is enough to demonstrate the idea. There is a round terrace located at the level of the entrance that serves as a continuation of the horizon. A table, also circular, and its chairs constitute the decoration. Added to this circle is a round cupola which rises along austerely cut pillars of massive volcanic stone that support the roof at an ideal distance to offer shelter, while stretching out to what is infinite. «You usually take a little from the outside, and frame it. You limit it, surrounding reality so that you don't get lost in it,» emphasizes the architect.

Laboratory of Styles

The kitchen is located according to its virtue of service, next to the dining room and behind the pergola. It does not scorn the panorama, nor does

Vault with movement, bricks that seem to travel in opposite directions without any apparent order, a simile of the undulating metamorphosis of dunes in the desert.

it invade other spaces or disguise its purpose. What's more, it prides itself on its presence in open agreement with the strong organic lines of the rest of the house.

In the kitchen, soft forms are evident in the maplewood of the cabinets and chairs. Each surface is carved, sculpted to the smoothness of a woman's tanned skin, full of life's healthy warmth. This in full contrast with the granite tabletop, a material used also on one of the walls,

rough and primitive, reminiscent of the cliff rocks that look out toward the sea.

Another World, Barely One Level

Steps below lead to an adventurous, playful site. The swimming pool seems to be on the verge of plunging over the edge, the terrace is set deep into the mountain, the master bedroom looks wonderful from all sides, and a Jacuzzi invites one to ritual purification. They seem to be pieces

of a puzzle not yet assembled. In reality, however, what Tapia, the architect, recreates in his work is drawn in a plan where a circular bedroom, the master bedroom, overlooks the sea for almost 360 degrees. The swimming pool is located on the projecting shelf of a mountain, opposite a terrace useful during strong rains or hurricane winds. The corner for reading is tucked away in the last bit of the property to distance itself from the possible murmur of other inhabitants.

«The architectural proposal must be addressed to people, and people always bite off more than they can chew. If the fit is right, we've achieved that wonderful feeling of shelter and comfort.»

Fortunate Guests

Casa Bashforth is also aware of its guests, with two private guest bedrooms, each of which looks out over the sea; each delights the senses with carefully designed furniture, lavishly detailed bathrooms. The central hallway of this upper floor is presided over by a pair of chaise lounges, apparent offspring of Botero which invite you to lie down on their raw silk upholstery.

«Rectilinear, but changing elements; the friendly proportion of materials are mixed with the dimensions of space. The result: spaces that transform themselves and transform their occupants.»

The construction gives refuge to its inhabitants and traps a piece of infinity for household use. It channels the splendor of the countryside, converting it into a manageable sensuality. Together with the architecture, the surrounding landscape makes this a lovely spot to live.

Form and Background in Open Complicity

The house is a polished jewel, its parts adorned in sublime beauty. It is a masterpiece in several senses of the word: for the site where it is located, and for being so complete.

Tapia endowed Casa Bashforth with a play of contrasts; antagonisms that subtly confront each other to prevent one from becoming totally lost in the sensuality of the house. Pillars are made of dark volcanic stone, of monastic appearance, of iron-like character. They sustain the explosions of soft, twisting forms. They represent the pretext of good sense.

However, prudence stops outside the door to the master bedroom: its circular plan «barely provides a visual control;» it inspires an explosion of fantasies as if on an extravagant stage. The bathroom becomes a shell, formed of small pieces of rectangular ceramic, with larger vitro-blocks of the same design on the other side;

the space grows up vertically to make room for the magic. «The height of the walls adds to the sense of balanced proportions; in large spaces with a view, the height of the ceiling is low; in smaller spaces, ceilings are higher to continue the sense of spatial harmony.»

Colophon

At Casa Bashforth, spirit is not captured, but expands, barely contained, thanks to the architecture of Próspero Tapia. People have the starring role, not the sea, despite the blue spilling through the windows. It doesn't trap the inhabitants, but allows many things to happen all around. There is incredible bustle in the house. Walls inspire; spaces dictate the mood; you breathe a different air. It is the sum of private secrets, of specialized spaces.

«Small» takes on a new meaning. Shared areas are of key importance in a summer vacation house, and in Casa Bashforth intimacy is important.

Casa Clark

Shy and Shameless

ÁVALOS ARQUITECTOS Y ASOCIADOS, SC
PROJECT AND CONSTRUCTION

Nine years later, Clark House looks as young and fresh as when it was conceived by Architect Jacinto Ávalos. It is the fifteenth of his constructions, the second in the Pedregal, and the first of real importance, in Ávalos' own judgement. It is 20 meters above the sea, seated along the cliffs, and blending into the tones of the rocks that support it. It is built onto the street, then hangs in the air, immune to erosion.

It debuts effects that the architect had only dreamed of, like rooftops converted into gardens or tapestries of marble. An anecdote accompanies its origin: the architect tells that the client was interested in a piece of land that had been called «unbuildable.» So he sought the opinion of Jacinto Ávalos, who assured him there was no such thing, and that the solution depended only on what the client wanted and how much he had to spend. The cliff in question was mostly air, but the architect was willing to hang his plans there. The client described his idea of the house, and Jacinto imagined the space. A few months later, a deal was struck.

When the plans were ready, Jacinto brought them personally to the client, thinking there would be difficulties of interpretation. He was right; the client refused his plans categorically. Jacinto asked for a corner in the client's offices and began to construct a model of cardboard, styrofoam, sticks and glue. He worked all night until he had a 1.5 scale replica. Seeing Jacinto's ideas take shape convinced the client to go ahead.

Piece by Piece

The estate is located on an irregular landscape of 64 by 15 meters. There are 657 square meters under roofs, and 355 square meters of terrace space, and a garden of 520 square meters. The house is striking from a distance because of the imitative tones that cover it completely. It is integrated into the morphology of the surroundings, it opens onto the sea, it extends from the landscape without calling attention to itself, but without losing its personality. «It adapts to the abrupt topography and accomodates the irregularities, respecting as

A frank presence on the street, horizontal without violating the surroundings. Imitating in its exterior the forms of the surrounding cliffs, unobtrusive stairways, terraces carved among the rocks, date palms which seem always to have been there.

much as possible the beauty of the rocks, and taking advantage of the views on all sides,» says Jacinto Ávalos.

Its circular cupolas, looking almost spherical, stand out and yet meet the height limits for the area. They have colored lanterns at their base which shine at night, and add an additional element to the interior by day.

Away From Prying Eyes

The house is far from anonymous, but efficiently safeguards its privacy. It has views from all sides, but none of its neighbors can see in. From the heights of the project, one sees roofs and well-

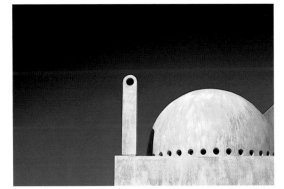

tended gardens. Looking from the beach, one sees a mass the same color as the rocks, and high windows which brook no invasion. The access from the ocean side is quite «conspicuous,» by means of stairways which literally lose themselves among the rocks.

The house achieves its ambivalence between extroversion and introversion: voluminous walls facing the street, its open and unmasked face toward the sea. «The architectural solution takes in all the angles, marks off and reinforces the vistas which will last for ever, and turns away from those which might fall hostage to fortune or the future. There was only one possibility of immediate neighbors, and that

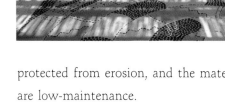

*Pure geometric walls: jelously guarding
the interior, and open to the sea.
Size that determines the level of privacy,
and dimensions which enhance
the surrounding natural beauty.*

*The vaults are circular, with lanterns
in their bases which repeat inside
the natural light outside.*

has been resolved by incorporating the nearby hill into the property of the estate, and planning for a new Ávalos project.

Intentions

Ávalos says that the design of the house conserves the majority of the natural elements of the cliff: it adapts to the topography of the landscape, to integrate with the morphology of the rocks. Also, the space is adequate to the conditions of the surroundings. The house resolves functionally the linear schemes which the cliff demands. It permits access from the exterior to each of the living areas and provides views of the sea from each of them.

The estate boasts only indispensable furnishings, minimalist decorations that enhance the relevance of the architectural space and their natural surroundings. Those parts of the land which are in contact with the construction are protected from erosion, and the materials used are low-maintenance.

Levels of Intimacy

The distribution of space in the house is simple, obeying the intentions and tacit rules of simple living. There are three levels in open harmony, in concord with the landscape. Areas are marked off, and each claims its own space and creates its own sensations: the breeze which passes through the living room; the tubular banisters which, like those on ships, do not block the view; the marine breeze which drifts up the cliff to caress those above; the sun which falls cleanly on the outdoor furniture; the swimming pool level with the horizon; and the dominant well-being and comfort of every area.

The first level, even with the street, has three entries: the wide, principal staircase, the servants' entrance, and the guest entrance. As well, they give onto the parking area, the storehouse, the gym, and the jacuzzi and swimming area.

The second level is a social area. It contains the high-ceilinged vestibule, the sitting-room, the dining room and the kitchen, the laundry room, the guest bathroom, a shower and dressing room, and various terraces with differing degrees of exposure to the sun. There is also a Junior suite, the servants' quarters, a larger laundry with an area for hanging clothes, the machine-room and the cistern.

On the third level are four bedrooms with respective baths, terraces, and gardens. The showers are on a mid level below the washrooms so that no one should miss a view. The rooms are crowned with cupolas, with their ever vigilant lanterns. Circulation among levels is open and easy; no one has to enter the central module to get to or from the bedrooms. The

arrangement is congruent with the flow of air, with an open tranparency of the windows and the privacy afforded to each dwelling area.

Uses and Customs

The Clark House manages different social, family and business purposes. One or two couples could live here without feeling lost in an mass full of doors and spaces. A gathering of twelve would be comfortable without disturbing daily events. A couple occupying only the Junior suite would feel cozy without filling all five living areas.

The space will accomodate intimate dinners or splendid parties. It can be used to attend to clients or business partners, or for a vacation with the kids, guests, and guests of the guests.

«It's important that each person be able to find a space, open or closed away, and not feel the necessity to mingle with other guests. The owner is generous, and likes to entertain. And so he conceived his house, proud to serve as a relaxing social space or quiet getaway. «Richness and multiplicity of space to accomodate different people, different groups, different ages.»

Theory

«We had to enclose in three areas the entirety of the project: first to fit the personality of the client, his needs, requirements, dreams; and second to take into account the natural surroundings— the climate, the structure of the land, the context; and third, we wanted to combine the two.»

In Clark House, Jacinto Ávalos has used closed walls, minimal openings onto the street, («to see but not be seen»), to the mutual benefit of all.

The house accomodates the topography, using the shape of the mountain, respecting its milenial form and adding to it, taking advantage of the 360 degree view that the location provides.

CASA CASCADA

FLOWING WITH THE TERRAIN
LIKE CASCADING WATER

DOUGLAS BURDGE, ARCHITECT
PROJECT

PRÓSPERO TAPIA, ARCHITECT
CONSULTING AND CONSTRUCTION

The entrance gate, wrought iron bird-of-paradise blooms in a verdigris finish, creates the first lighthearted touch. Following a pebbled path that leads to the house's various levels, the burbling of water leads us to wonder whether the waterfall flows around the building, or *vice versa*. There's no sound of the sea: surf noises are superseded by the running water near at hand. Stones in the stream are moss-covered, giving them a venerability that belies the house's relatively recent construction. The waterfall can be regulated to gently trickle, flow steadily, or rush effusively: though it passes through the interior and out again at the building's lowest level, it gives a deceptive impression of having the sea as it outlet.

Challenging Limits
The local residential community stipulates incorporation of three design features: arches, white walls and red roofs.

When the owners said they weren't particularly interested in arches, Architect Burdge designed some to be unassuming: unembellished, they seem to evolve from the rocky foundation. From above, they form a V-shape; seen

from the ground, spans of Roman arches extend from the parking area to the entrance corridor, fitting the community's requirements, but taking a rather pompous stance.

At first, Casa Cascada is not easy to visually take in: its rooms are concealed by the mountain and by the property's foliage, lightly sprinkled by the waterfall.

Up the main stairway, the view is diffuse; finally focussing, at the top level of the waterfall, on the platform for the house's swimming pool.

High contoured walls roofed by tiles reveal nothing of the activity within; large windows encased in a heavy wood that suggests ancient ship construction add to the mystery.

Neither modest, humble nor fussy, the house declares its weight and boldly limits incursion, save by wistful glances through huge doors, at the massive spaces within.

The interior proudly keeps its distance, and keeps to itself: its rooms are not built to welcome the stranger, nor his idle gaze. Instead, they are designed to be enlivened, transformed and lightened by the family and their friends.

When the mood strikes, Casa Cascada metaphorically loosens its armature of glass and

Mexican-style arches and roof tiles were required elements for Casa Cascada's construction in its residential complex, but were not exactly what the clients had in mind. Architect Burdge worked out an ingenious compromise, and the result is an engaging home whose magical waterfall duels with the sea for attention, the sea conceding a draw at day's end.

wood and revels in the deliberate disorder of its rambling terraces. The sound of moving water is ever-present, its force custom-regulated.

Each living area is designed to function, and to function autonomously. The dining room/kitchen's heavy wall-length wooden «curtains» open, to be harbored in wall-recesses; the area revealed is unexpectedly large and striking. Filling the wall opposite the window, a large sculpture; between, a long table lined with handsome chairs.

What can be seen of the woodwork from this vantage is dark, and undulates around the room: it curves lingeringly, traces organic forms, eschews straight lines in the veneer that flows over doors. At the far end of the room is a spectacular metal and blown-glass sculpture, reminding one of a gnarled tree.

Beside that is an artful bar that serves the courtyard, with decorated ceramic tile portraying the very view it looks out upon: a kind of Borges illusion, infinity caught between mirror images.

Large windows go beyond wood and glass: each is also custom-fitted with shutters and mosquito netting. Even with the added volume of these remarkable and functional additions, window treatments can be completely recessed into the walls.

Once Again, Inspired Order

The adjoining building has the same windows, another living room, a bar. Foreswearing austerity, furniture is carefully selected, seemingly uncoordinated, scaled-down, in a testament to convivial individuality. Several «*miguelitos*» (a kind of chair), are interspersed amidst brass tables from India: the sofa is Empire style. Once again, magical tendrils of wood

wander: contrasting with its dark tracery, the ceiling is covered in light maple panels. With the bar set at right angles to the room's squareness, one wall — with leather and rattan benches, and two original portraits of women by Cauduro — becomes the focal point.

Striated stone pillars reach to keep the ceiling from seeming to rise too precipitously. To these supports are fitted wrought iron frames for fabric screens, which add warm waves of texture to the room once the window blinds are tucked away.

Two stately doors open into a home theater, upholstered throughout in coarse neutral-toned material to make seats and aisles unnecessary. A table, made of fir beams, supports audio and video controls.

In the bedrooms, furniture is simple, but there are state-of-the-art means of controlling light, music, air conditioning and visual effects. All bedrooms overlook the sea from a terrace: the mood is distinctly Oriental, with bamboo mat ceilings and desktops. Each provides a range of different sights, all within the same panorama.

Mindfulness

Locally quarried, unpolished stone, rustically-set apricot marble, and impressive multi-toned woodwork are elemental. The railing along stone steps by the steep waterfall is a single organic shape in verdigris-finished metal. As the railing descends, all the way to the beach, banisters become soaring stylized seagulls.

Dark wooden blinds lend a serious, introverted mood; when these are drawn, and completely hidden in the walls, the house becomes a series of festive terraces.

Set amidst primitive stone, a coquettish wooden bridge crosses the spring that flows through the interior. The swimming pool above is Venetian mosaic, in azure shades that mirror sea and sky, from stark white to midnight blue.

Despite its massive proportions, the entire house bespeaks voluptuous sensuality. Its garden, at the lowest level before one reaches the beach, has lush pineapples and other tropical foliage set within a green lawn. A jacuzzi and bar are secreted beneath the center of the house in a kind of rocky cave.

Guiding Concepts

The owners purchased the land for Casa Cascada in 1994. James Burdge, who designed the mansion they built here, says, «When you go on vacation, it's important to really be 'elsewhere and otherwise', so I developed upon a concept of being simultaneously indoors and out, with no harsh demarcation. As my plan followed this concept, each room was designed to function independently of the rest.» The area for socializing, as the most important, is at the very center: this also allows for choosing whether you will get together with others in the living room, dining room, kitchen, inner courtyard, or at the swimming pool. Other areas of the house, in his vision, would be placed in the background; «One central building and separate rooms all around.» The owners like Mexico and Mexicana, but not «colonial» style — preferring more Polynesian architecture.

With future neighbors also in mind, the house has a private, inward look. Each space is graced with a view of the sea and, in the foreground, the garden: otherwise, the view is internal and indifferent even to the nearest outdoor features.

All the comforts of a Hotel

Utility and comfort were designed into a plan that would accomodate owners and guests: there are several bar areas and kitchenettes.

«I thought of it as a small, private hotel for very special 'guests', among them the family members. A successful beach house is one with enough hotel-type dynamics to allow carefree access, along with the freedom everyone wants sometimes, to go off to rest or read a book alone.»

Not a house requiring much movement between upstairs and down, you can arise in the morning and stay busy downstairs until it's time for bed: in between, if you need to return, there's even an elevator.

As to the waterfall, Burdge comments: «It doesn't compete with the sea: depending on wind direction, the ocean can sometimes be heard. But the waterfall is always here, with its three speeds lending verisimilitude and charm.»

Outdoor illumination creates interesting attractions after dark: when, unlike the guarantee of ongoing daytime events, visual effects must be engineered.

Casa Cascada embraces natural woods that range from Brazilian walnut and mahogany to window casements of the wood used in Pacific shipbuilding.

«At the end of a time away from the house, whether the intervening month or so has been good or bad, we wanted all the materials, colors and textures here to be imbued with a sense of pleasant return.»

The house flows toward the beach with the same liveliness as its own waterfall. Stone steps descend amid vivid vegetation.

Casa La Favorita

A most mexican home

Byrl Binkley, Architect
Plan and construction

Built from shared impressions and earnest communication, Casa La Favorita crosses aesthetic barriers to achieve its lively style.

«There are two ways of describing one's house: the first addresses its sheer beauty, the quality and tastefulness of its furnishings, its spectacular garden and view. The other, more emotive description, focuses on the contentment that living here brings: 'Look how happy I am to be home'», as architect Byrl Birkley says.

For Byrl, success can be measured by the daily delight clients feel living in a home which was once only an architect's plan. Throughout the process of realizing his plan, he elicits the owners' ideas, moving with them through the rigorous construction process, painstakingly situating everything from their initial wishes to their future daily lives within the home's walls. For him, this is the essence of residential architecture.

Definite Tastes

At first, La Favorita might be set anywhere in Mexico — somewhere, perhaps, in the colonial city of Guanajuato or the Los Altos region of Jalisco. The hermetic facade with its narrow windows belies the «music» that lives within, placing the house definitely in Los Cabos.

Its walls are white with touches of terracotta, and a paler clay-tone on casements.

Entrance is through a gate to a traditional patio, full of flowers and greenery, with a central fountain. It is a private «plaza», where fun and fiestas await family and friends. The patio is the owners' favorite tranquil place for morning coffee; here they can start their day amidst bird-sounds and the scents of earth and vegetation.

Sitting on the patio, it is difficult to imagine the house being set in Los Cabos, atop a rocky cliff — though easy to know it's in Mexico, as every detail, floors, furniture, art, utensils, is 100% Mexican.

Magical Chameleon

After coffee, fruit is offered. When a guest crosses the threshold to the house's interior, he is stunned by its difference from where he has been. The inner structure is consciously, breath-takingly transformed by shades and shades of deep blue, an amazing seascape.

At first glance, Casa La Favorita could be anywhere in Mexico, perhaps in the colonial city of Guanajuato. Its unassuming facade, the murmur of the patio's fountain, the house's narrow oblong windows, all belie the majestic ocean views from within.

Although the site's elevation is no mystery after one has climbed the winding street that leads to La Favorita, one doesn't initially imagine how steeply the house sits on a cliff above the waves, how daringly close to the sky it appears.

One is also struck by the solidity of its exterior: and the visual irony of its strong presence against the seeming fragility of anything that faces the «void» from the cliff overlooking the immense sea.

Amidst *talavera* (majolica from Puebla), equipales (rustic leather furniture), cupolas and hand-woven textiles, the house celebrates Mexican artisanry from throughout the republic: but it is undeniably a house by the sea. Blue is everywhere: glancing back toward the patio, one now sees a stripe of sea through the windows.

«One of my main concerns was to be 'within reach' of the ocean from every angle,» says Byrl, and this challenge he has clearly met.

Authenticity

While the owners and architect are from the United States, they show clear preferences for Mexican design. They exhibit respect for Mexico's artistic wealth, and have immersed themselves in her culture. This house has been built as a monument to Mexican visual arts, and a testament to gratitude for their life here.

La Favorita is set on an irregular 800 square meter plot, much of it dramatically

elevated. The house covers approximately 450 square meters.

The feelings the house inspires in the owners are profound, best expressed in their anecdotes about its creation, the importance of having been part of the process, their relationships with the people who built their home. They introduce some of the workers who continue to be part of their lives, and the life of the house. Among them is José, who has just been working outside: for many years, he has been in charge of La Favorita's maintenance.

Traditional Mexican arches face the horizon, and bougainvilleas surround the pool area, placed at a dizzying height above the sea.

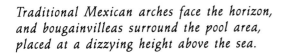

It is a house full of favorite spots. When the lady of the house tries to choose one, she lights first on the kitchen, with its interior and exterior views: the private warmth of the entrance contrasted with command of the sea. Another, of course, is the patio, so suited for morning coffee: and in the afternoon, the pleasures of the terrace. But also there are the office, the bedroom, the bathroom — all complementing one another, each with its own temptations to linger — making the choice of just one special place impossible.

La Favorita is distinctive not only in its *mexicanidad*, but in the ways it highlights Mexican details. Unlike most Los Cabos

The house's scale adds whimsy to the setting's drama: stone pillars and a substantial roof nevertheless seem to float on the cliff.

swimming pools, for example, which look out over the endless sea, this pool is elegantly, intimately surrounded by bougainvillea. «The sea is out there, but the pool is in my garden,» says the woman of the house.

Space is delineated simply, and functionally. The main space, under its cupolas, encompasses the living room, dining room and kitchen. This area is itself surrounded by a wide terrace, with welcoming rustic leather chairs.

The main, and only, bedroom is spectacularly simple, mixing visual magnificence and a sense of seductive privacy.

The couple speaks of the whole house as if it were a loved one, thanks to Byrl's vision and implementation of this special commission. He explains that he learns what to attempt by listening to the clients: his spatial solutions develop out of their work together. When they disagree on occasion, solutions are negotiated point-by-point.

Byrl credits his clients with knowledge of Mexican architecture, and a strong sense of their own style and preferences. Working from their wishes, he converted the space into walls, surface finishes, a complete custom environment.

A number of cupolas are part of this environment: featured in the bathroom, bedroom, living room, dining room and kitchen, they look down on interiors full of careful attention to detail.

The Owners

«I don't understand why people come here and build houses that may as well be in San Diego,» says one of the owners, noting that the kitchen is the only room where her dedication to Mexican interiors has been adapted, as she does the cooking. The kitchen opens onto the living room, for sociability while she prepares meals.

Confidence in the choices made while building the house has grown: «If it were to be built again, there's not one thing I'd do differently.»

By building a small home, with one bedroom, she thought maintenance would be easy: but living by the sea means endless toil. The window-washer barely finishes the whole house before he must begin again.

She thinks of Mexican architecture as somewhat formal, and well thought-out. «Use of bright colors doesn't mean that it should look like Taco Bell,» she says, and cites examples from her own and others' homes.

She gave the architect total authority in designing the bedroom. «And I never imagined,» she says, «that he'd be able to create such eloquence

and intimacy by judicious placement of cupolas and niches.» There was a difference of opinion over the bathroom, as she wanted a room built to the larger, U.S., scale. «But I learned, and adjusted, and the result is what you see here.»

The carved wooden headboard, bought over thirty years ago in Hermosillo, is just one of the pieces that have accompanied the couple throughout their shared life. The stone horses that watch over the pool have already «lived» at two earlier residences.

The Architect

Byrl is measured in his speech, concise while expounding architectural concepts and sparing in talk about himself. His goal of satisfying the clients with the structure he's made, day to day and over the course of years, allows him to think even beyond beauty and functionality. He quietly and very modestly accepts recognition when his work enhances the spirit of those who live in Birkley homes.

For him, there are homes whose beauty derives from an array of beautiful objects, tasteful decorative ideas and luxurious materials; there are others that could contain a single simple chair and still proclaim their beauty. Architecture is about placing the owners at a point on this scale that provides them a true sense of ease with their surroundings.

His philosophy is one of dynamic simplicity: his houses are never ostentatious, nor does he crave celebrity for himself. It is important to him that his clients awaken each day with renewed delight in their home. When he finishes a project, he and the clients have built a valued friendship: for him, this is the most crucial proof of a job well done.

The patio dazzles and draws the eye; charged with its own magic, it gives no hint of the interior's impact.

Wrought iron, stonework, ceramics inside; strong walls protecting privacy, and nothing outside suggesting a beach house. The true function and materials of the house are revealed by looking beyond the surface.

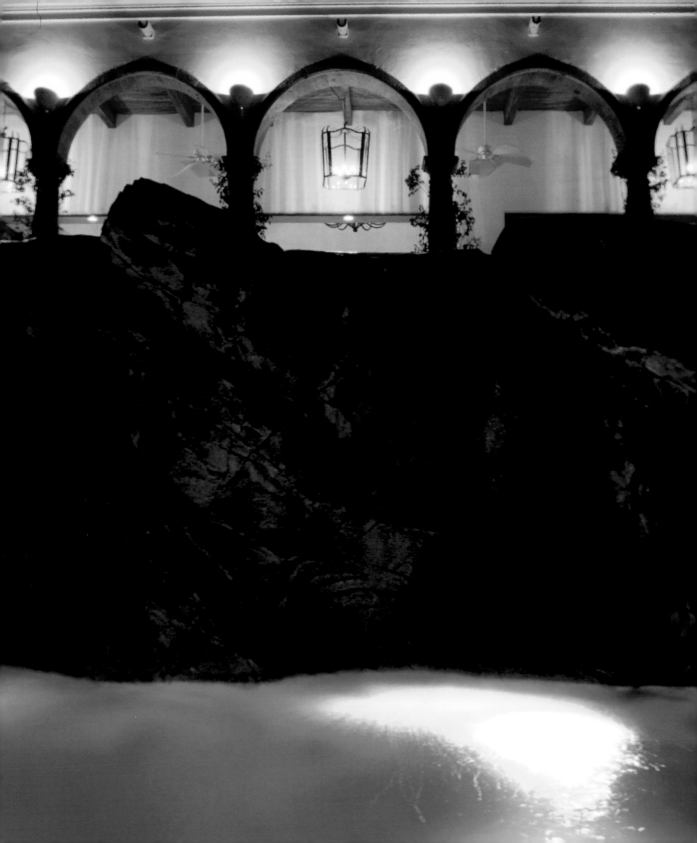

Casa Encanto

A festive spirit of shared pleasure

Pedro Meza Servín, Architect
Project

Constructora Malver
Construction

The young owners of this house wanted a home full of tradition as well as playfulness, set in a wide landscape and affording the comfort they knew they could create within its walls: they trusted its exterior would blend with surrounding domiciles.

It is an interesting mix of hacienda, ranch, beach house; of private, festive, sea- and land-borne modes; of natural and man-made vistas.

The entrance hall has a stone floor, *palo de arco* ceiling, and wood-encased windows. There is an old-fashioned passage-way, leading in both directions to bedrooms, creating distinct family areas, each with its own patio.

In the central archway, the door opens upon the blue spectrum of the interior. Expansive and eloquent in its exterior visage, inside it is a deep luminary vestibule which steps down into the living area.

Detailed wrought iron borders stone floors, as sumptuous as well-trod woollen carpets.

Casa Encanto is comprised of three buildings: one for family life, a barn of a space in the center which looks out over the two areas that are used more after nightfall, the bedrooms.

Living room walls are defined by chair rails all around, and wooden beams delineate the ceiling, creating warmth within magnificence. Such details also reflect the residents' spirit, bringing the enormous room into human scale. Bedrooms beyond strive for the intimate, restful proportions of dreamscapes.

Nobility

The central structure's nine by fourteen meter floorplan is divided into living and dining rooms and kitchen, under a single roof which rises from 7.5 meters, to a peak of 8.5 meters. A series of small windows along the high wall provides indirect, evanescent light. The kitchen has its own lowered ceiling for privacy and visual intimacy.

Casa Encanto's wished-for «age» was hastened by an artist who «faux»-painted the marks and cracks of dampness and natural seepage over the years, upon the walls. If dampness were to enter here and there over time, it would just blend in with the artwork.

In such a purposeful vacation home, the exterior is crucial, but should not be imposing.

An entranceway with rock pillars, its stone flooring appearing more like filigree in the lofty living room; more arches on the terrace, frame Casa Encanto's splendid garden. Attentive decorative details inside lend distinction and warmth.

Thus, massive square-paneled doors humbly stand free of distracting hardware, folding inwards to permit access.

Shared Intent

Roughly finished, walls mimic the uneven surfaces of historic buildings. There are stone columns in the wide corridor which serves as a terrace: these don't obstruct the view, but, by virtue of being natural, highlight and fine-tune it into an image of solidity against the mind-boggling horizon.

The storeroom floor, like the patios, is aged quarry stone «for greater character», and for natural continuity between inside and out. No frames or borders nor even the subtlest detail announces the line between interior and exterior.

Here in Casa Encanto, the gaze never quite knows whether it's landed upon the ceiling or the sky itself, and the sea shimmers in both.

Natural materials are used throughout: wooden beams and palm fronds, quarry stone on kitchen and bathroom surfaces for congruence.

«Masculine» in its exterior qualities, the home's character seems even stronger and richer indoors, with an odd sense of being a «youth hostel for grown-ups». Festive, frank and open, it is ready to receive guests, as many as it can hold. There is also a sense that the house knows just what it has to offer those guests.

The objects inside contribute a feminine aura: «trifles» that are hardly trifling, they give an impression of having been here forever.

Furniture is comfortable and anything but intimidating; its style, age and materials have

The main building hints at a nineteenth century barn or granary, but here it is human creature comforts that are addressed. Decor declares the family's talent for placing well-selected pieces, each in its ineffably «just right» setting.

all been specifically chosen for everyday use. Additional elements —paintings, carpets, lamps— naturally coexist as background. Bedroom curtains, for example, are large expanses of the fine cloth known as *manta del cielo*, suspended from strips of cloth attached to wrought iron rods with mother-of-pearl buttons. In their delicacy, they look as though elderly seamstresses sacrificed their eyesight upon this labor of love. Superb hosts, the owners express their generosity of spirit in the excellent harmony of their home's decor.

The kitchen appliances, climate control and pool equipment are all state-of-the-art, causing a departure from the rest of the home's «heritage», but they bring the comforts of the first world and the next milennium.

Bed chambers, especially compared to the living room, are small and country-style, closed against the bustle of the world. Bathrooms share this mood, but while small they are proud — if not vain — in their luxurious details. Even the sinks appear to be made of delicate lace: these showpieces were rendered on-site in ceramic.

As in each of the buildings, exposed beams support the ceiling (and weight of the roof tiles) from wall to wall. The polished cement floor is intentionally speckled to age its surface; the door frame is stone. The large bedroom areas have patios, sanctuaries at some distance from the communal space. Stone stairs leading to them are detailed in wrought iron, with niches and lanterns to add interest and light.

The office of the «lord» of the hacienda is an enclosed studio with a terrace overlooking the sea. Furniture here is over two centuries old, and it is indeed authoritative.

Behind the study is a children's room with whimsical bunkbeds where up to six youngsters can rest after an exhausting day in the sun of the beach, swimming pool, or by the waterfall.

The Owners

Pedro Meza, architect, and Miguel Ángel Arce, engineer, together created Casa Encanto, with one doing formal plans that would be implemented by the other. They agree that the house successfully aims to look older than its five years, and proud of itself. «It does look wonderful from all sides, with great views from all angles of its 360° and 100% Mexican panorama,» Meza says.

It also abounds in visual delight: no matter where you turn, your gaze unconsciously finds design elements full of Casa Encanto's personality. «Some architecture is impressive for its grand scale or dramatic tones,» says the architect, «but Casa Encanto is impressive for the human joy it imparts.»

And the engineer agrees: the client wanted a typical Mexican house set in Mexico, but totally different from Mexican-styles built in the U.S. Though they wanted a «hacienda», the topography, with relatively shallow frontage on the street, balked. Thus, three large spaces — two for bedrooms, with a communal area in the middle — were placed about the property.

The architect and engineer take us through the basic construction stages: first, retaining walls were built and the land filled, with rocks and earth from the property moved around as needed. Then the land was graded in preparation for the foundation. «The rustic stone floor was incorporated into the plan as the project proceeded. The ceiling, of *petatillo* or straw matting was treated, and brushed with linseed oil, to discourage insect infestation. The windows that face the entrance hall are reproductions of historic examples, crafted by local carpenters.»

They also have anecdotes from the project: the owners wanted the main door to be distinctive, and a search for a suitable piece began. The house was finished without having found the perfect door, so an interim one was created.

Made of Abeto Douglas wood, its surface design combines both pickling and combing with special tints, on top of which wax is rubbed. The iron hinges and other hardware were forged here in Mexico. Then, the clients insisted upon rustic wooden windowsills, and untreated stone, despite the area's dampness.

Finally, when all the design challenges were met, they were delighted with their home.

Large-scale, yet attentive to minute touches, with masterfully-resolved elevations and well-tended gardens, Casa Encanto's details are graciously expressed in everything from imaginative «aged» finishes to the shell buttons of its delicate living room curtains.

Casa del Cielo

House made of sky

Ego Construcciones, SRL de CV
CONSTRUCTION

Diseño y Construcciones DYC
CONCEPTUAL DESIGN

Alejandro Álvarez Guisa, Architect
PROJECT DEVELOPMENT

Elías Gutiérrez Osuna, Engineer
CONTRACTOR

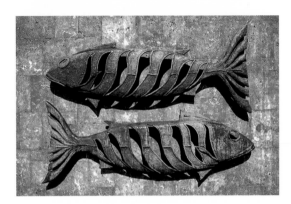

The dimensions are generous, to say the least: living room, dining room, kitchen and terrace are located inside an ample perimeter, with high ceilings and windows which look towards a proud seascape. It is the only house in the Palmilla development which has been built on two lots.

The turnaround at the entrance is presided over by a Zamarripa statue, converted into a fountain, which greets the visitor as he arrives. The door opens, and one discovers that the sea, in all its expanse, has become a visitor in the living room, so large and spacious is the room. On the principal terrace, fresh water makes its appearance in the form of a jacuzzi, which also serves a fountain, its water running to the lower level over a wall. A wet and constant, calming murmur runs through the house, itself made of just the right materials which turn and fold upon themselves with majesty.

Raison d'être

The generosity of construction is unlimited, each detail keeps the same key. The kitchen, for example, uses wood inlaid like that of a fine guitar. Behind carefully made wooden screens are the refrigerator, freezer, and fuit and vegetable bins.

The kitchen counter is dressed out in metals which are repeated at the bar. Stars seem to shine from the metal, at times outdoing in brilliance their originals in the heavens. Elías Gutiérrez Osuna, the contractor, describes Casa del Cielo with full knowledge, without missing

It is a thematic house. Its name is not capricious; each room expands on a section of the firmament: the moon, the sun, the sky. The circular entrance represents the celestial carpet, covered by a cupola, a vaulted chamber.

a detail, an anecdote, or the degree of difficulty of each element, obvious or hidden, large or small. This estate, he says with conviction, is «one enormous detail.»

For the Chosen

The universe of the entrance opens onto two corridors, both in finished cactus, one open, the other behind glass. The wings lead to the three bedrooms. The first is in a lunar theme, with all that evokes. The headboard has a moon in a niche, repeated in the lamps of the bathroom, in the mosaic of the washstand, and again in the interior patio. Another bedroom is done in a sun theme, with similar results.

Arriving at the bedroom of the sky, the stars multiply in porportion to the space they cover. Everything is bigger: a celestial, spatial hierarchy. The room appears to be a house apart; it has a small gym, a jacuzzi with a view of the sea, closets, larger windows, and an enormous bathroom.

One glass covered corner gives way to the work corner of the lady of the house; there, the blue of the sea, the sun, the moon, the stars evoke the creative impulse of a free spirit.

A Private Exterior

The roof of the principal sitting room is peaked. The higher part is seven meters. A beam makes it less imposing. The entire front is of sliding glass. Two columns of local stone arch over the entrance vanity; warm to the touch, agreeable

to the eye. Behind them is a half bath and the family entertainment center. The first is sombre, its ceilings high, the second breathtaking in its demensions and technology.

The grand and open terrace follows on from the entertainment center. It roof is in the shape of a pergola, or dome, with a clear barrel vault. It is the passage that announces the transition from interior to exterior. The «social» jacuzzi is located in the center, one of its pipes leads to the lower level like a fountain, over the wall, and feeding into the water that supplies the swimming pool. Nearby is a large telescope. There is a thatched roof over part of the swimming pool and a bar. The two levels are marked off by a large beam of original design and splendid manufacture. A game of circles and scantlings which does not impede the view but rather gives shape to the landscape.

The estate has controlled lighting, well thought out and programmed. Indirect light, reflectors, modern fixtures. Lumination which fits the design, capable of modifying the volume of space and outlining particular areas. Exact in its intentions and expert in fulfilling its function.

Wood, Metal and Stone

The quarry stone floor is inlaid with red fragments along the borders. There are only a few steps in the hallway and another few to reach the sitting room. The windows are sliding aluminum which converts the room into a covered patio. Cosmic themes in metal adorn the

bed, illuminate the bath, shine in scenic reproduction, all controlled by computer.

Each bath, besides their ruling star, has a special touch; from the tiling of the wash basins to the design of the showerhead. The moon and sun rooms are brother and sister in location, personality and hierarchy. They do not compete, but show off without jealousy. The sky room gathers strength from all the natural elements without going beyond «good taste.» It is clear that this space has the power of the cliffside, imposes terrestrial laws on domestic operations. Two stairs lead to the bed, a picture window prevents the sea winds from disturbing the peace.

In the bathroom, the niche and cover for towels and equipment are of thick Italian glass, a transparency which defies gravity, suspended as if by magic. The doors and closets are wood, higher than normal, finely worked and smoothly finished. Doorhandles and knockers denote sobriety and service. But where wood as a material of choice really shines, is in the kitchen; here, it proudly makes of this normally humble area a pround adornment of the entire house.

The metals adorning the bannisters mix sculpture and utility, to amaze and delight with a confusion of usefulness and beauty.

Running Water

The first water one encounters is the fountain at the entrance; Zamarripa has made it flow, running down the stone which gives form to his magic. The head, sombrero and clothes of metal remain dry, while the rest of the mass is darkened by water. The murmur is barely audible, the sensation is only lightly perceived, the beauty is conclusive.

The next water which appears is the square terrace pool, at times calm and tranquil, at other times bubbling playfully. This flows over to the next level in an eternal play of falling water, in neverending waves.

A bronze Pisces hangs from a wall where the water falls from the jacuzzi; a pair of fish always provocative in their tones, always changing with the water that slides continually over their scales. The work is unique, designed by Julián García and cast in Mexico City.

There are two small gardens, an ode to the surrounding desert; each cactus is an excellent example of its specie and the sand is the finest that can be found. Two great rocks stand like brazen desert prophets. The swimming pool is on the next level, static when no one is in it, the only thing without movement. Water, architecture, grand spaces, and the stars for constant guide. A house which goes beyond its original conception, and acheives eloquence.

Details and Quality

Casa del Cielo is itself one great detail; it manages with mastery its vast dimensions, and at the same time specializes and delights in the small

and minute. It needs no dressing-up, no extra furnishings or decoration. Casa del Cielo is adorned by the perfect use of material, by their clever placement. It is complete in its view, its metals, its stars and its purpose.

Wrought iron screens, raw linen curtains, beds with views of the sea give the house a special style. Every door is of finished oak, giving onto the terraces as far as the laid stone allows. The pipes are painted copper, so that, even unseen, they do not interrupt the color tones of the faucets.

There are constants which give continuity to monumental spaces, without stridency or abrupt changes. Here in Casa del Cielo, the fan windows are the same in all rooms; the materials mark off each space, with distinct dress, but identical in essence; the lighting assures a beauty and an artfully concealed vanity.

In few words, Casa del Cielo is peacefully clothed in magnificence, in tranquil opulence, luxurious rest, but without demanding of undue attention. Their subtlety is assured by the gentle murmur of waves.

Airy in its grandness, adorned with detail, dressed in simulated simplicity; here circle the stars, here the heavens are reinvented.

Casa Cerro

An estate that sums up the landscape

Julio López
PROJECT AND CONSTRUCTION

It hangs off the mountains, dressed in their tones, encrusted in the rock as in a natural cradle, embryonic. It springs up from meters below, where the street runs, but the journey really begins from above, in an undisturbed terrace which embraces an entire horizon, the only refuge the solid mass behind.

The floor is red, the circular bench is protected beneath an arbor, the barbecue ready at a moment's notice. The parabolic antena is camouflaged in the surrounding rocks.

Fragments of a House

One arrives by an interior stairway, through an insignificant doorway which gives no hint of the leisure behind it, or the tranquil dawns it witnesses. Flowers outline the grandeur and entwine with the sighing breeze.

The first lower level has two bedrooms with a wide hall between. Each thinks itself the showcase, each guards jealously its privacy. They are decorated simply and soberly. They share a terrace, spacious demensions and high ceilings. The hub of the stairs is cylindrical, with windows; one descends without losing sight of the view, without forgetting the blue of the sea. The motif of transparent circle is repeated in the kitchen, and gives form as well to the swimming pool, the overlooks, the jacuzzi.

The principal entrance and the the sitting-room are located on this level. Wrought iron and metal cover the vanity at the entrance; outside a fountain murmurs. On one side are the dining room and kitchen, as well as service areas and a half-bath for visitors. The space is duplicated in the exterior, which widens as if trying to reach the horizon, restrained only by the mountains.

Magic Temptation

The swimming pool is scarcely restrained, it appears ready to join its waters with the milenial salt waters of the ocean. It glides in a smaller circle, completing the optical game of imminent

It is elevated on the hillside, and then lowers itself slowly in a smooth descent. Its four levels house four bedrooms, three terraces, and various lookouts. It imitates the rocks which support it, and follows the game of their form and tone.

escape. Curtains are pleated, not hidden away. The patio lounges reign supreme, the barbeque as prince consort. A stairway, this one external, leads below to another house, encrusted with the rocks of the hillside until it seems part of the landscape. A neighboring bedroom occupies this additional space. The mirror of the washroom gathers in the two infinite blues of sea and sky. Decoration is in clear colors, whites with flashes of other tones, preferably sky blues.

On the other hand...

A wooden screen is tucked cleverly among nearby trees. There also are the first steps which irresistibly catch one's eye. At each turn, at each new level, one is caught by surprise. Watching one's step, one discovers a floor of cement set with fragments of broken red ceramic. Thirty-six stairs lead to the first scene: a wide patio with rooms around it and the fullness of a swimming pool at its center. Eighteen steps more and the

One terrace crowns the estate,
a space which takes the full measure
of the spendour of the surrounding
landscape, and testifies to its grandeur.

The rooms are pale, mixed whites and blues which smooth the interior and colaborate clearly with the nature of the exterior. There are ample patios which invite one to leisure, to contemplation, to the simplicities of life.

entrance fountain appears, in an area covered by an arbor of tree trunks.

Crossing through a shady space, one comes to the ample sitting room which gives onto the living room, dining room and kitchen. A small exterior stairway leads to the main terrace. Here is the pool, whose form is as capricious as the stairways, wooden beams, and hallways. The dining room window, a rounded, horizontal rectangle, takes shape in a pronounced curve of wall. The living room is quite small; it privileges the mountains and sea. Any seat affords a magnificent view.

The mirrors of the bar multiply the heavens and the seas. From here arises another series of steps, covered by a cylindrical hub of the same materials and designs as the exterior version.

The level spaces fall in syntonic arrangement with the design of the mountain. Each one has a patio which enhances the pleasure, and the view. None is without its interval of leisure, its own small piece of the dawn.

Nineteen steps lead to two bedrooms, one white, beige and pale green, the other, white and blue. The general colors of the house are pale and calm. One door seems to lead nowere special, but that is not the case. There again are the stairs leading up. Twenty one steps up the mountain to the top of the estate, to the platform which crowns the cascading levels, which fall gently towards the street.

The estate repeats the rock tones of the surrounding area in its walls; the blue of the sky and sea in a variety of details; the capricious forms of the mountains in curved spaces of the house. Repeated as well, throughout various parts of the estate, is the local vegetation. Four levels make up the universe of this house, each unique, yet part of the whole.

Casa Dos Hermanas

A cosmic reordering

Ávalos Arquitectos y Asociados, SC
Project and construction

Jacinto Ávalos brings together in the Two Sisters the best of Mexican architecture; he synthesises great space, generous walls, mass and sun. All without excess, and gifted with balanced color, detailed joinings, and careful treatment of color.

The sitting rooms give onto a principal patio and the center of the house's gravity: the living room, kitchen-dining room, the terrace. A fireplace sits in plain view, in the coldest part of the house. Is its significance mystic, poetic, or purely practical? Mere presence, or source of heat? Reinventing the exterior elements, it reaccomodates them to a human scale. It is the reordering of the cosmos, repeated indoors, the poetic side of architecture.

It is not a window on the sea, it is a house in the sea. However, the water is not seen from all angles, it must appear of its own accord. There is always the possibility, but it choses its moment. Nor is there a desert exterior, but it shows in the texture and tone of the walls.

«Architecture lives in time, runs in it, intuits it, discovers it,» says the architect.

Narrow Streets and Plazas

The point of departure is the planning of needs and tastes of the clients. In this case, sisters from the United States, with a deep appreciation of typical Mexican style. «The house brings together living in the country, and living by the sea. In a place like Los Cabos, one adapts to the surroundings,» says Ávalos.

«We wanted to emulate a small town. The patio is the main plaza, and the three sitting rooms which give onto it represent the public buildings. The narrow streets are here the stairways which lead to various houses, or rooms.» He adds, «There is a hierarchy of space, from the most private bathroom, to the bedroom, to the private terrace, and thence to the completely public.»

«When one is in a vacation home, what one wants is change, something different from the customary. If not, it's not a vacation. One of the changes is the presence of other people, relatives or not, with the consequent friction, since each one has his or her own idea of recreation. So they have to be houses that offer

This house is a synthesis, and a cleansing. It is an estate of one story, a hollowed out monolith, austere, with studied care for detail. It matches the sober magnificence of the region.

multiple spaces for people to enjoy in different ways, to seek out, at any moment, a sense of well-being and harmony; if you find it, you relax, you're on vacation.»

The entryway is a filter which impedes passage of strangers. It is a vestibule that distributes people in certain directions and not in others. From here one goes up to a terrace or down to the central patio. Its fountain muffles conversation, blocks the invasion of more intimate spaces. It is a filter in more than one sense. It also gives onto a separate bedroom,

apart from family or social comings and goings; separate. That's the idea.

«The house is a continuity of privacy,» says Ávalos. One of the walls of the living room is a remembrance, a testimony to the perimeter fences of the property. It has, also, a skylight which gives enough light to compete, in

Here the senses are fed until satiated: the views of the surrounding landscape are delightful. The murmur of running water and the smell of the herb garden next to the kitchen, arouse and delight the senses.

constant and vibrating motion, with the sun's clarity. Without it, the living room would seem, from outside, to be in constant darkness. Jacinto says that this arose from the need to add texture, and to create contrast. «I live among rational, intellectual architecture, and it is often tedious, or cold. So one must balance it with more natural, rustic elements: columns of tree trunks, adobe, pergolas. They give a certain friendliness to all the mass and geometry.»

The adobe of this panel keeps perfect harmony with the walls of the rest of the house, in two tones: a white base and a stained surface. It evokes older, warn, centenial walls. With all the skill of hard use without showing the effort. The double tone recalls the ambivalence between rock and leather.

The materials of the house are conditioned by a practical aspect, although they do not deny the underlying intentions of caring for the well-being of the inhabitants. The floor is quarry stone and marble, for example. It stays cool, doesn't scratch, isn't slippery, and cleans easily. It's durable. Its presence in every space constitutes a constant theme throughout the four-level estate. «Things should have meaning; if they do, the design has power. If not, there is only collage.»

Meanings are in Details

The central patio boasts a fireplace. Says Ávalos, «Most people feel that a house is incomplete without a fireplace; especially those from the

The external elements are echoed in the interior, in useful form, for the comfort and service of those who live here. Nothing is fortuitous, everything has a purpose.

North. For them it has enormous significance. In Los Cabos a fireplace is almost pointless. We solved the problem by putting one outside, since there are many months of the year when the outside temperature is rather chilly.

So the central patio creates a delightful «sweet and sour» of heat and cold, and makes sense. Even when it is not very cold, the reflection from the fireplace through the entire area creates a most agreeable sensation.

Also, as part of the «curious conceit» of emulating a small town, we needed a tower. It is the pivot, or juncture, which separates public and private space, where one turns to walk along

the narrow streets which lead to the scattered rooms on other levels below. «One of the important characteristics of home design theory is that they should seem introverted from the exterior, in full contrast with an extrovert interior. This is important for this house in particular, given the view that it has.»

One encounters the surrounding landscapes at the turn of a corner, descending the staircase, or looking out from the terrace: rooted trees, fragments of the sea, stars without end. «I want the inhabitants of the house to be able to

do whatever they want wherever they want, without neighboring estates limiting their activities.»

What You see Is...

The facade of the house is blind, but has its own expression; it speaks volumes. The structure generates spaces, and these arise from the foundations. It is honest, sincere. «I like to use materials that give a sense of volume,» says Jacinto Ávalos who has a preference for terraced roofs. On this estate, one is a terrace, the other a garden.

«I don't do double walls, I design the space in such a way that the closets, the bathrooms, and the doors give the impression of thick panels.» As well, «I am interested in framing views so that other homes are not in the sight line. People come here for the natural beauties of the area. We like to give them that without

obstacles.» So an inoffensive tower has been raised to block the view of neaby construction. Thus the house is completely the Two Sisters'; well thought out, carefully and intentionally designed, without being obvious. Like a beautiful woman's makeup.

«The lavender blue of some of the walls appears a reflection of the sky and sea; it is included in the interior so as not to contradict its exterior extravagance.» Also, he confesses, it's his favorite color.

The details of the house represent a concern for excellence, the fine thread that runs through all of Jacinto Ávalo's work. Hangers for the hammocks, ladders of woven reed that serve as clothes line, wooden lattices which hide the air conditioning.

Nothing is excluded from Ávalos' plans. For every activity he designs a space, for each sentiment he creates an area, like the niche on

one of the stair landings dedicated to «reflection, to looking beyond one's self, to communing with the spirit, a place of contemplation.» Or the finish on the doors, an arch in the middle, filled by a stained glass representation of the region's most typical tree (the *Torote del desierto*) in two versions: in color for the exterior, and the same design, but transparent for the interior doors. As part of the tree there are two circles (the sisters) and smaller circles (other family members.)

You have to live it

Two Sisters is located on a cliff subject for most of the year to strong Northwest winds. The sliding doors allow for the changing weather. Jacinto Ávalos is familiar with nature and adjusts his designs to it in consideration of the inhabitants of the houses he builds. He brings nature into cooperation with the building.

«Nobody loses a view; no matter which chair of the dining room you chose, or in which part of the house you are, there will be a beautiful view of the sea.» Not only is Jacinto Ávalos concerned to maintain the vista, but he wanted to reduce the intrusion of outside noise by neutralizing it with the gentle sounds of circulating water, by means of a small channel which carries a stream that passes by the dining room and falls into the swimming pool.

In the other garden, lower down, close to the kitchen, there are herbs and spices. There, a nearby bench invites one to sit and lose oneself between the distant sea and the immediate fragrances. «There are things you can't photograph. You have to live them. There are lots of buildings that lend themselves to photos that are nevertheless difficult to live in.» That's not the case with Two Sisters.

CASA LA PALOMA

DARING, WITH CLASS

GRUPO MCA. ANTONIO CARRERA, ARCHITECT
MONROY ARQUITECTOS. MARCO A. MONROY / JOSÉ M. MONROY
PROJECT

GRUPO MCA. JORGE CARRERA, ENGINEER
CONSTRUCTION

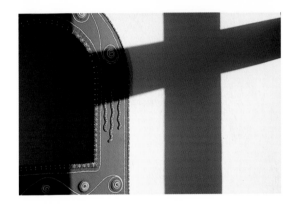

The building is white, smooth, honest. The sea is nearby, as it is for all houses of Los Cabos, but in this case the sea seems almost the continuation of the patio, which in turn seems a continuation of the sitting room. The architects Carrera and Monroy, who had charge of the project aimed for freshness, enthusiasm, even a touch of insolence. The owners, Lennie and Jerry Berkowitz, have allowed their house to strike a note of discordant harmony in the neighborhood.

The spatial hierarchy is perfectly democratic, in dimension, landscape, and comfort. There is a marked divorce between the social area and the private area, a division of necessity, and taste. The play between verticality and smooth undulation is a constant. Even more, it could be called the principal characteristic of this house.

A year and a half old, 400 square meters of construction on a 1,500 square meter lot, and a frankly contemporary style describes the Casa La Paloma as a living being, young, and fresh. Its style converts it into a constant provocation in the neighborhood by virtue of its simple form and clean lines.

The owners, 76 years young, enjoy the house. The architects, Carrera and Monroy, also young, knew how to embody the restlessness and needs of a family which enjoys the convenience of separate bedrooms.

Antagonisms

One enters the house via an ample, descending staircase. The house is on a lower level to accomodate the height of the interior without exceeding the limits imposed on construction in the Palmilla development project. The mischief

Youth defines the Casa La Paloma. And a certain insolence is added to its destiny, completed by a mixture of straight lines and sinuosities. Contemporary without restraint, simple at all costs. A taste for the Mexican is present in the exquisite decoration, an indication of knowledge and sensitivity.

begins at the front door, made of old wood, as are the handrails, which are no more than studied grooves in the walls.

Crossing the threshold, one enters an agreeable home, completely white. Three stairways of organic shape lead down from the vestibule, or rather, announce that one has left the entryway behind. Walls become shelves, niches, tables, chairs. Whiteness lends itself freely to interruption by sharper, brighter colors.

The flight of the roof continues over the terrace, with no indication that we have left the interior. The view that opens out towards the sea pays no attention to almost nonexistent fences, or the entwined branches of the pergola, which tries vainly to contain an ephemeral house, living by its own choice in complete subordination to a glorious landscape.

Inside, there are the necessary walls in the usual places, but living room, dining room kitchen and hall are without frontiers. There are two master suites in each wing of the central building, four rooms exactly equal, but on different levels.

Contrasts

«The idea was that from the entrance the house would be inviting, open, without rails or armor,» says Antonio Carrera. He adds that «in keeping with height regulations of the area, the estate sits as low as possible.» Thus, almost three meters of gentle stairway leads down to the entrance.

«The main idea was to manage neutral colors on the larger surfaces: white walls, clear gray stone on the floors.» The brighter colors are in the details. There are no in-betweens,

no half-shades, no ambiguities. Things are, or they aren't.

From any angle, the Casa La Paloma plays a good game of mass versus lightness, an insolence of contrast, verticality converted into smooth waves.

Its whiteness does not make it different; it is the simplicity of its form and cleanness of its lines, its frank contemporary style which confers distinction upon it.

Natural Composure

Its particularity, as well as the cleanness of its lines, is found in the adornments, which contain all the colors of the Mexican craftsman's rainbow. Lennie and Jerry Berkowitz know this art well, they have travelled in Mexico for over 40 years. They have always known they would retire in Los Cabos, always known as well, that their house would be furnished with select artesanry. More than a dozen alebrijes placed carefully on shelves welcome the visitor, with the Sea of Cortés as backdrop. Multicolored chairs

of Scandanavian wood, designed by Arne Jacobsen, are placed around the antique table. The bar is hidden behind paintings by Antonio Vivaros, which form a kind of naive mosaic. Huipiles with embroidery of silk, and platters from Michoacan adorn the walls like the true works of art they are.

The wide windows of the main sitting room are built into the walls, removing any obstacle to the patio and the sea beyond. Only a few subtle marks on the floor which do not interrupt the freedom of sight or of human passage.

The open clarity, and the clear gray stone of the swimming pool, support the sensation of free passage. A small border of stone marks the boundaries of the property. The kitchen is small, well integrated into the social area.

The strong colors take life in the furniture, in the decorative peices, in the details. Good taste is present everywhere and balanced in a perfectly natural order.

The roof is almost three meters above the floor. It seems higher because of the direct line of the clean white walls. The television room, also part of the social area, has a vaulted ceiling perceptible only to those in the room. Without a hint of shame, the patio is adorned with palm. Clear quarry stone, a small swimming pool and a small pergola adorn the large platform.

There is a pool in the garden, so there is no lack of the sound of running water. It is a particular mark of Los Cabos houses, that they like to compete with the sounds of the sea. Lennie and Jerry Berkowitz have been involved in various building projects in the United States, but without doubt, their house in Los Cabos is their favorite.

The Berkowitzes consider that their architects, Carrera and Monroy, have been skilled interpreters of their dreams, and have managed to give them a creative and imaginative form. The engineer, Jorge Carrera, was responsible for converting the architectural project into reality. The house is the result of close teamwork.

Protected Privacy

The client, the owner of the house, wanted private bedrooms, far from other, public parts of the house. This was achieved in two bedroom areas, one at each end of the central module, with one bedroom on top of the other. These four are the main bedrooms, with private terrace and bath.

The verticality is constant, the guideline of architectural design; the smooth waves invite themselves in, pinnacles of organic form, sensuality made walls. In the background, the sea is a constant companion.

If the house were a hotel, the sitting room would be the lobby, restaurant, bar and guest suites. These are not large, but sufficient close to the social activity of the house, although the «routine of Los Cabos takes place mostly outside; it is difficult to remove oneself from the friendly climate and beautiful landscape.»

Those same nine feet down which one walks to enter the house, one mounts to enter the two wings of the house, via hidden staircases, with smooth steps, and a quiet passage.

White on White

The contemporary conception, and the tastes of the owners themselves, chose white as the base for everything. Walls, ceilings, internal and external lighting, even the wooden doors are finished with a faded white.

The handrail of the stairways, sunk as they are into the walls, is a contribution of the Carrera-Monroy team. As well, the sofas in the living room, the armchairs in the TV room, the low walls for flower pots, and the stepping stones. It is an architecture which enjoys details of decoration. Platters which give something extra to a wall, convert a room into a comfortable living space. It is a project which aims for more than simple arrangement of space.

Casa del Faro

Radial geometry, an echo of the horizon

Próspero Tapia, Architect
Project and construction

The road is not inviting, it resists interruptions of the enormous silence. But beyond a hill and after a sharp turn, one comes upon the Faro House.

A complete surprise

It is a play of contrasts, riddles, almost jokes. It mixes the interior and exterior, public and private, strength and delicacy, covered and desert. It has youth (it's only three years old), but wisdom enough to sit peacefully in emptiness. Mischievous walls in contrast with the open horizon: here a wall of certainty, and there the open sea. All the traditional elements, but set out here in a new, radial geometry.

The first level is desert, the second the bounded depths of ocean. But when it rains, the Faro House seems to have moved from some other place, from distant climes. Its surroundings change, and greenery covers the formerly dry plains.

«Using all the given elements, we tried to construct a spirit of place; in this case a pleasant spirit.» In these few words, the architect Próspero Tapia, sums up the intentions which brought this estate to life. «The system of construction makes it special. It's in the old style, but adjusted to modern times. It arises from its foundation without arches. But it's not utilitarian; it's real.»

It is hidden away; the hillside keeps it a secret until just the right moment, at the last turn. «The idea is to discover it in stages, given its geographic location. And within the house, as well, to discover in stages the enchantment of its different areas.»

The idea was clear from the first conversations with the client: a hacienda entrance, a doorway reminiscent of the great country estates, away from the crowds. The house was begun three years ago on four thousand square meters, which might as well be thousands more because of the surrounding desert. There are 400 square meters of construction, which seem to multiply since the interior gives so readily outward. And 400 square meters hardly contains one as does a normal house.

Tapia mentions the regional materials which were used: «Young quartz, plain rock,

The proud expanse of the land has an impressive impact. The distant sea is present as a difuse line of land's end. The desert is in full spendour; hills of stone, an arid, uncultured, wild horizon. There are no neighboring constructions, not even scratches of plans in the sand presaging future inhabitants.

which makes a nice contrast with treated textures or sand and river rock. These are natural elements which speak with their own voice and imitate the surrounding area.» A colonial oasis.

Radial, like the horizon

The dwelling is oriented in such a manner has to never face obstructions, and since the neighboring area is natural drainage, it is highly unlikely there will be other estates.

«The view radiates from the house as from the center of a circle, past two beaches toward the Western Arch,» says the architect. «It's identified with the old lighthouse, with Land's End, and has a studied and enjoyable solitude. It fits into the area like an echo.» It not only fits, but participates in the dualities of heat and cold, inside and outside, rock and crystal. One side is covered, quite functional; the other opens generously outward. There is the pleasant sensation of sun 300 days per year, with accompanying and abundant shadow.

Contrast, and sense of play. From the landscaping, the strength of construction, to the wooden beams which cover the doors, there is a sense of playful contrasts. One is invited within, or thrust outdoors, there is no midway. The idea is to be a part of the surrounding land, part of its comings and goings, bi-directional.

It is open, but when one passes beneath a deep shadow, the ambience changes. In spite of

It hides shyly among the desert mountains, sheilding its personality until the last turn, apprehensive until the last moment. And then throws off all composure and gives itself entirely.

being directed outward, the sense of interiority is heightened. This is one of the successes of the estate, according to the architect. A wise selection of old Mexican material serves modern needs admirably, like the granite of the kitchen, which accomodates comfortably the high-tech gas and electric installations.

The Hacienda Takes Shape

The Lighthouse Estate remembers Colonial Mexico, integrates it into an open, flexible plan. «It meets the needs of today, and allows the older, colonial, architecture, the romance of stone, to remain a reality. This one can accomplish when one has such distinct spaces to work with.»

The client wanted a hacienda, and it is decked out as a hacienda. First, with a great front door, at the top of a set of radial stairs. The sitting room is a central nave which hides nothing; from the door to the beach, crossing the desert, the spatial comunion is complete. It is a construction which has simply occured upon the landscape.

The kitchen follows the same pattern: it leads to the dining room, without walls or disguise, and thence to the terrace, and then, without previous notice, there is the sand and the sea. The pergola is a great rudder; «the owner wanted to feel that he directed the destiny of his house,» but more than that is the sense of place, so that one feels integrated with the space, «otherwise, one would feel as if he were floating.»

It is a strong house, which provides security without concealment, but open, enjoyable. «It has the structure of a 16th century convent, improved by technology,» says Próspero Tapia. A beautiful paradox of strength and lightness; sheltered and open to the elements at the same time.»

Changing Seasons

If the weather demands it, the house hides its interior, and wears its outer face. If the wind rises, the windows, like hired hands, gather round to protect their employers, without obstructing the magnificence of the panoramic views.

«The winds determined the execution of the project; great mass is required to tame them, to create a certain dynamic that allows the wind currents to move around the building, without remaining completely outside, otherwise you would battle the heat.»

The construction is well defined, and limited to the requirements of the dwelling. Within the term «openness,» Tapia adds the notion of «repetition,» referring to a series of small windows which provide intermittent views of the mountains. The front of the house gives onto the sea, the rear exterior opens by pieces, symetrical and repeated. They are like anchors, since finally what a dwelling must do is give

It has the form of an old hacienda; from the main entrance the portals seem señorial, awaiting the return of the patron. It lives in dignified contrast with the desert, the mountain, the sea.

protection. More precisely, a support, a sense of belonging in a very special place.» The area is remarkably pleasant, but one needs a place to come home to.»

Space, ambience and function

The social area is made up of terraces; these are treated as points of transition. One senses that the kitchen is the house's center of energy, the the generator of all activity. If there are few for dinner, they sit at the kitchen table; if more, in the dining room; and if even more, they spill out onto the terrace.

Sliding doors around the perimeter give the house a contemporary dynamic. They make an open place, in spite of their conservative nature. The master bedroom repeats the visual game with its contrasting wooden closets and modern windows. It evokes a pleasant air, but with a

frank smile; and invites a person in with warmth and solidity.

The bath adjoins the bedroom by means of a median arch which allows it to keep its secrets, but holds a reading chair as well. A festival of intimacy, of open spaces which hide secret sites, without doors or walls. Fun. The shower has a space of its own, as does the bath and steam room.

The lower floor has not forgotten that it is part of a colonial estate, nor does it abandon its vocation as a beach house. Wood and sea, protective walls and large windows. Thus converge three houses, to include the two dwellings of the sons of the estate. This achieves various objectives. It marks off space, age, activity and quite readily forgets them all when the children take over. An ample house for a couple, and receptive as well to guests.

Ticks and Details

«Spectacular construction provokes a certain fear, an anxiety. A house for living should gesture towards the human scale of things, and provide security.» Thus was born the Lighthouse Estate. It is not so grand or imposing, but makes proper use of space, dimension and material, «to join the sheltered inner house to its exterior.» A basic value, after all, since the client paid much more for the interior than the exterior. «And this is very important, since at the moment you open the door, the house multiplies.»

The same elements that are outside are repeated or reinvented inside, in an interaction, not only of colors and textures, but of the rhythms of the landscape, the objects that catch the attention, that arrest the eye. «One has to impose limits, since, after all, everything has one.»

Casa Cambells

A dream on the crag

Lorenia Riva Palacio Delmar, Architect
Diseño y Construcciones DYC
Project

Luis Raúl Romo Carrillo, Engineer
Diseño y Construcciones DYC
Construction

The natural surroundings presented a challenge: there was a difference in elevation of 15 meters between one street and the next. We were to construct a house, precisely there, that could live in harmony with the Sea of Cortés, the Pacific Ocean, and the desert mountains. First, we had to convince the owner, and keep our feet on the rough terrain at the same time.

It was an act of imagination, to dream of a house higher even than the cliff, so the sea would expand to spectacular vistas. And Mrs. Campbells wanted a Mexican house, including patio. Fortunately, the area included a tongue of land, with a triangular wedge at one end.

Imagining the Space

«Without much level land to even stand on, we had to convince the Cambells that the dining and living rooms could become a reality, from which they would look out at the Pacific and the Sea of Cortés; that the bedrooms would be quiet enough, with only a strip of ocean, rather than a beach full of chattering bathers below,» recounts Lorenia Riva Palacio, the architect in charge of the project.

She adds that Mrs. Cambells insisted on the patio, but there was only 15 meters of width to work with, and a few more at a lower level to make up the total area. «The solution was a walkway crowned by a very Mexican arch, which leads to the swimming pool and fountain; it serves also to join the bedroom at one end and the kitchen and living room at the other.» The long corridor is warm and inviting, thanks to the use of just the right materials and decorations; at its mid-point it opens to the street as well as to the garden. The corridor widens to almost the entire width of the property, and thus creates the patio proper. There is room for a terrace adjacent to the living room

This house came into being through tenacious and imaginative will. Not only was the terrain difficult, oddly shaped and uneven, and surrounded by streets, but we wanted a view, peace, and spirituality. The finished house is called Casa Cambells.

as well, which gives onto the quiet beach, the very antithesis of the noisy oceanside resort.

The corridor, or walkway, has a double function: one exterior, covered by arches at midway, and giving onto the patio, swimming pool, and the mountains; and one interior, with windows onto the street and the main door at midpoint. It is finished on one side with an old painting of the Archangel St. Michael, and on the other with a mirror. It is a long corridor, almost 30 meters, but the decorations give it a liveable air, which the material would not

normally allow. The columns of the arch preserve the color and texture of quarry stone, although they are, in fact, concrete. The floor is in the Saltillo style, with a narrow strip of authentic quarry stone.

It is a one-story house, ideal for a couple: bedroom, living and dining room, kitchen, terraces and patio. Seen from another angle, a wider perspective, there are two guest houses. At a lower level, and completely independent, are the apartments of the house and grounds keepers.

Rocks without Threat

A grouping of rocks in the shape of a cave is on a part of the Cambells' property; Lorenia wanted to keep it as a natural masterpiece. It is large enough to be habitable, but she refused to build

Its Mexican character was achieved through volatile flights of imagination, combined with the determination to figure out how to locate a house on a parcel of land with fifteen meters elevation difference. What were simple lines of blue on the horizon have become magnificent panoramas of the Pacific Ocean and the Sea of Cortés.

the house «around the stone.» She resolved not to touch it, to respect its integrity, and to build on either side: above, the main house, and below, the guest houses. Her idea was seconded by Raúl Romo, the engineer in charge of construction. They are part of the estate, rugged in shape, warm in tones, and pleasing in dimension. The house was finished with a large window framed in limestone, which is repeated as frames for the mirrors on the closet doors. The result is a pleasing effect of stone and horizon — repeated, extended and reinforced. The visual field is freed, and sways gently from the rocks to the sea and back again in endless amplitude and beauty. The impression is of a bedroom, larger than its simple measure would suggest.

At the lower level, where the two guest houses are, the cave becomes utilitarian. It makes space for one of the bathrooms, and becomes part of the whole area, dedicated to family and friends. Although the Cambells like their peaceful and intimate privacy, they also enjoy having guests.

The Personalities of Space

Mrs. Cambells, Mert, has a spiritual side, an aspect of her character that wants to make use of areas in the house for reflection, introspection, and meditation. For Mert, the peaceful quiet of the afternoon, the natural harmonies of the sunset, and the tranquil appreciation of other hours of the day, led to certain architectural concepts about the use of space.

«The project required the creation of certain sensations, rather than particular types of space,» says Lorenia. «The house had to be for both Mert and Tim, with their differences and similarities, the mystical and realistic, and sufficiently intimate, even on a bluff surrounded by streets.» This was achieved by means of elevating the land,

so that even with streets nearby they are not seen. A powerful architectural fantasy, born of the Cambells' confidence and Lorenia's professional clarity, imagined the terrain and allowed to walls to go up.

Making the Dream Come True

The original challenge became titanic when we considered more deeply the future inhabitants of the house. «Not only a harmonious, Mexican house with a view of the Pacific, the Sea of Cortés, and the mountains, but a space with the

special sensitivity to life that the Cambells share.» The land was unforgiving. «We had to use small spaces to contain and express the large openness that the Cambells were looking for.» Lorenia remembers:

«There was hardly room to stand on both feet; the seas were simple lines on the horizon, the walkways were far from the center of the estate, above our heads even.» Thus began the dreaming: words came and went; the Cambells talked of needs, customs, habits, while Lorenia talked about space, area, or materials.

The long corridor, of almost thirty meters, is warm and discreet thanks to a careful use of materials. It has the job of uniting the living room-dining room with the main bedroom. Midway, it opens onto the street and the garden.

Details

The house reconciles different customs and activities. The swimming pool is large, since Tim likes to swim daily. One of the sides of the pool, which looks over the street from a considerable height, is a beam from which fish hang in mid air, necessary when children are near the pool. Tim likes iguanas, Mert is less than fond of them. The solution: «Some low rocks near the dining and living room must have been the iguanas' original home, so we raised a structure over them and left a pair of iguanas there.»

They can only be seen from the street below. Tim let the process unfold, and waited for months for the dream to become reality, a house they could touch, and live in.

For Lorenia, «architecture isn't about building something that fascinates you, its knowing how to join a particular piece of land to the desires of clients.» She tells of finding Mert on one of the terraces one morning, exactly as she had imagined her. «My work is to interpret the desires and needs of people, to look at things from their perspective.»

Casa Karina

Designed for daily living

Víctor Cauduro, Architect
Project

Vission Custom
Construction

Planned from the beginning for family living, this home's spatial organization emerged in response to routine moments, activities and, naturally, need for security.

Even down to the calm neutral colors chosen throughout, the residents' life — laughter of young daughters, talk and music enjoyed within the family sphere — takes precedence over the sea and the exterior views.

Architect Victor Cauduro worked with Luis Cano, owner of both the property and the construction company which built the house, «responding to the family's ideas from the very first sketch.» Cano continues, «We tried to maximize the view, without sacrificing the interiors: we wanted this to be our lifelong home. We think of it as 'Home', with a capital 'H'.»

It began to take form, and to reveal its purpose: not even the entrance gate is shy about stating that it's all about home, security, family.

From the entrance pond to the wide garden around the swimming pool, the house presents interesting details at every turn, calling the children to play throughout a space that is tho-

roughly Mexican in its interpretation of Colonial Californian style.

The architect originally pictured surfaces in white; later he and the owner decided on a harmonious range of sand tones as being «warmer, and more liveable.»

Casa Karina's textures are also distinguished for their «studied indifference»: beiges play tone on tone in varied materials, creating a mosaic in high- and low-relief.

Spatial Discourse

Expecting to see the ocean right away, one is instead presented with another panorama in the vestibule — still aquatic, and no less enchanting, but standing on its own as part of the home.

It is a home in every sense, without zany or strident spatial statements, clearly and frankly committed to sheltering the family. «Here I am, home at last, with everything just as it should be. What more could I want?»

Casa Karina's grace comes from all that happens here: its walls would be nothing more than aesthetic ways of dividing space were it not for their place in the lives of the inhabitants.

This is a house in a privileged setting, with its ocean view, spreading garden, ample spaces; it is also indisputably a young family's home. Nature's spectacle takes second billing to the house's domestic role: splendid functionality exists within beautiful surroundings. Casa Karina is a full-time, not a vacation, home.

Luis Cano believes that, «when one pushes limits, or 'shows off', one loses the simplicity and joy of creating a space made-to-measure for living.» His agreeably-proportioned home was completed in January 1999.

The right site

The house was built atop a high cliff, not on the beach: «I prefer to see the ocean, rather than be right next to it. On the beach you have the movement of the waves, but up here, away from them, you find more happening.»

The terrace is where the family feels most comfortable. «We certainly use this area most, and always together.». The family eats, spends the afternoon, and greets the evening here: a pattern shared with other homes in Los Cabos, and «why the terrace is large in relation to the interior,» adds the builder, who has sought (and sucessfully found ways to) bring the view inside.

The living room is formal, as is the dining room. The television, room with its large screen T.V. and overstuffed chairs, competes with the garden terrace for attention: and only occasionally wins.

No area is off-limits to the three little girls: «We want them to learn to care for things, by using them.»

As for his own favorite spaces, Mr. Cano unhesitantly mentions the flowing pool at his home's entrance. Its liquid murmur evokes for him his childhood home, set near a stream. He wanted to reproduce a sense of being sheltered and protected through the soft fall of water, and his wish was achieved after just one setback.

Neutral beige appears in every material: with different tones, textures and purpose, but always in harmony with family life.

Initially, it was possible to see the water through stationary glass, but it could not be heard. In order to bring the sound inside, he designed special fixtures which allowed the glass to be tilted upward. «Without this other body of water, all would be the sea, and it would force the attention outwards.» The house's own stream becomes a serendipitous counterpoint to the crashing sea, and a focus all on its own.

To avoid extraneous discussions about furniture, the Canos hired an interior designer to elicit and respond to their various tastes, interests and practical needs.

Meeting Needs

The image of the sea slips in and out, but it is not the highlight of Casa Karina.

The outer wall is of *braza*, a dark and dense volcanic stone native to the region. In the small garden which conceals the entrance, the man-made stream's small waterfall extends a greeting. Entrance is through a hall and a Mexican patio, and is visually arresting; large ceramics seem to float above the stream as it crosses the entranceway to settle in a specially-designed square basin.

From inside, each of the cardinal points is represented by an exterior view: the garden in two directions, the water of the pond to the front, the ocean at the fourth point.

The living room's ceilings are more than three meters high, with wooden beams. Its furnishings are formal, but not solemn; the large casement windows opposite the fireplace may allow the sea's presence or not.

The square tiles of Travertine marble are rough-edged to give the floor character: they also provide the perfect coolness to bare feet as the family bustles through the house.

All woodwork is American Adler: windows, frames, kitchen cabinetry, beams, drawers, closets, desks and bookcases. Their colors add to the gamut of sand-tones throughout.

The dining room is serious, classic; crowned by a high cupola from which its chandelier is suspended. Tall chairs covered in deep beige are arranged around the table, and the room's elegance is open to the kitchen, creating an inspired balance. The kitchen's central island is topped in Santa Lucia granite; underneath is space for keeping dirty dishes out of sight as they wait to be washed and replaced. The stone

Not a beach house, though it doesn't deny the ocean's beauty as seen from its garden: it is a home in every sense of the word.

«command center» accomodates the baby's highchair, the hostess and her friends chatting over coffee, the family and staff's gatherings.

Next to the kitchen is the laundry area, and the housekeeper's room, which also adjoins the children's wing.

The only room that was added to the design after the plans were approved was the family room: it was important to have a place to be together indoors, as well as on the terrace. Without another place to happily interact, family members would have to go off to their own rooms.

The girls' televisions are used only for video games or taped movies. The «official» television is in a room where friends also gather to play dominoes: if it gets late, they may leave by a door

that takes them around the house, on a path where the sounds of their footsteps are well-muffled. The television room also holds a small office for the man of the house.

Design Honoring Family Routines

Finishes, like the use of stone throughout the home, eliminate excessive care or maintenance. They also celebrate a sense of permanence, or agelessness; the owners wanted the stone to appear to be «at least several decades old.»

It's easy to be in Casa Karina's interiors; each everyday routine is at home here. «All we have to do in the course of a day gets done faster, and more enjoyably, here.»

Its decor is homogenous, with touches that personalize spaces according to function.

Security and beauty live together here, as does wrought iron with the ephemeral lucid pool, roof tiles with the nearby desert, solid wood of ceiling beams with the rolling ocean.

Texture is a constant, as is color. The whole range of tans is here, from near-white to deep tobacco-tone.

Dimensions of each room also reflect function, alone with the philosophy of Casa Karina's creators.

The master bedroom is large, with two armchairs creating an anteroom. The bed is set to one side, creating its own realm.

Here, marble gave way to the owners' fancy, so the room is carpeted, but in the same color as the stone in the rest of the house. The ocean appears through small rectangular country-style windows.

The large bathroom's striking shower contains an illuminated niche displaying a glass-and-bronze fish sculpture. Another bit of magic is that a regulator heats the water to the owners' chosen pre-set temperature. There's no shower curtain or sliding door; a fixed sheet of glass prevents splashing beyond the shower area.

Here also, disguised as a framed mirror, is a closed-circuit camera that allows each zone of the house to be checked without interfering with regular television reception.

Two marble-topped sinks have drawers which hold not only appliances, like hairdryer and shaver, but the electrical outlets they require.

Mr. Cano's dressing room faithfully follows his regime: there's the bench facing his sock drawer, and a towel holder right where he might finish drying his feet, with all adding up to planned assistance for each stage of his toilette.

His wife's dressing room is equally customized: shapes adapted to specific objects, containers for every accessory and garment. The space is designed for the quantity, height and size of shoes, hats, belts, skirts; long, mid-length and «definitely short» dresses. Karina's dressing room was the only area where Luis' opinion was not elicited at all — though «I even offered my suggestions for her kitchen» — here, she was completely free to «design her own space.» Here also was the only adjustment that had to be made to the plans — an addition of eighty centimeters.

At the other end of the house the girls' rooms — with living room, kitchen and a kind of «art gallery» hallway in between. The design was unstinting in consideration of the smallest family members: steps for reaching the top of the closets while they «grow into them», and to comfortably use the sinks; furniture ready to hold computers, complete with shelves for keyboards. Theirs are rooms that will evolve into the functionality that's required at each stage of their lives.

Casa Quaccia

Formality in the middle of the desert

Gilberto Lares Moreno, Architect
Project

Constructora Malver
Construction

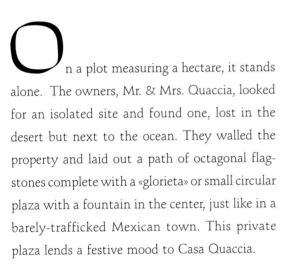

On a plot measuring a hectare, it stands alone. The owners, Mr. & Mrs. Quaccia, looked for an isolated site and found one, lost in the desert but next to the ocean. They walled the property and laid out a path of octagonal flagstones complete with a «glorieta» or small circular plaza with a fountain in the center, just like in a barely-trafficked Mexican town. This private plaza lends a festive mood to Casa Quaccia.

The entryway maintains the Quaccia personality while blocking access, declaring itself private property — not that there are many likely passers-by.

Gilberto Lares Moreno, the architect, drew up the plans and Miguel Ángel Arce, engineer, took on the construction, including all the technical challenges that arise: water, drainage, electrical installations, air conditioning; the basic issues of costs, energy sources, and transporting materials to the site.

A U.S. solar energy firm was hired to go over specifications, and they determined that all energy requirements, including air conditioning, could be met by the sun, with the help of a few generators. «Go ahead and design everything as if you had electrical energy,» they advised.

The engineer then had to plan construction costs, with few in the way of precedents for his budgeting. «Just having materials delivered to the site, on the other side of a fairly deep ravine, automatically made it more expensive,» Arce tells us. He adds that they had to set up a camp with its own canteen and bathrooms even before starting construction on the garage and caretaker's residence. From beginning to end they were «an experimental endeavor, a 'pilot project', which involved constantly monitoring complications, obstacles and costs.»

Three buildings, the home, garage and powerhouse, now stand on the Quaccia's land.

A hectare of nothing but desert; with no neighbors for kilometers; a deep ravine that must be crossed to reach it. Here the Quaccias decided to build their combination ancestral mansion and colonial ranch, admidst bare mountains and golden sand, and facing the blue sea.

127

The powerhouse, built near the property line, holds gas tanks, generators, the antenna for the radio telephone; solar panels, batteries and converters; and a reverse osmosis system for converting salt water into water for drinking and other uses, including watering the gardens. Once the outbuildings were situated, construction of the main building began.

A large gateway is the property's only access: it opens onto a drive which ends in a plaza facing the Colonial/California-style house. It rises from an elevation well above the beach, and is reached by organically-inspired stairways whose forms mimic the desert's shifting sands.

The house is actually two; a guesthouse and the family's domain, which blend into one another architecturally but are completely differentiated by decor, dimensions and functions. For both, the Quaccias' decision was

It requires nothing more than what it has: paved corridors, pillars supporting their palm roofs which provide shade and ocean views. «Lost» in the middle of the desert, Casa Quaccia finds itself elegantly at home.

to build «beach houses», but without bringing the beach inside.

The architect received a variance to combine more delicate arches, and partial arches; and to have certain areas which instead used columns of concrete, plaster or quarry stone; rectangular portals with or without molding; flat as well as peaked roofs.

A stairway marks the center of the main hall, one of its walls punctuated with windows that admit the lovely view. Three chimneys, serving the living room, master bedroom and

studio, rise above. After visitors have passed through a grapevine-decorated door, and under the house's only cupola, the open and welcoming entrance hall draws their gazes skyward.

One of Casa Quaccia's paradoxes is its accomodation of such a warm interior within a stark and immense exterior. Looking in through small windows with dark casements, the view is of formal furniture and built-in cabinetry in fine woods; elegant objects and Persian carpets. The home's mission is clearly to protect its inhabitants from temporal worries.

In the living room, a massive fireplace framed in quarry stone presides over gatherings, while a columned niche holds a sculptured Aztec bust, and large sofas in natural colors and fibers make themselves at home here. Lit by a finely crafted onyx chandelier, the dining room carries on the theme of spare elegance: in measured lines and tones, in its obvious aim to permit the assemblage of excellent furnishings and decorative elements to function as a whole.

In contrast, the guest house, in its frankly «country» decor, invites guests to take a relaxed and free-spirited vacation, away from reminders of city life.

It has one bedroom, a living/dining area, kitchen, bath and terrace. The living area also converts to sleeping quarters, with three beds that pull out from the wall.

Decor is informally, festively Mexican; with leather chairs, *talavera* ceramics, and colorful tones throughout.

Here, quarry-stone columns and wooden beams suit both the exterior and interior. Though it is just a wall that separates this from the

One of the three buildings holds the machinery that allows the home to function far from any urban center: pictured below are the solar cells, the reverse osmosis de-salinization plant, the generators and solar batteries. All of these help to provide the Quaccias with luxurious isolation.

main home, their interiors and evocations of the guest house are decidedly different: the prevailing feeling is one of being cared for, by kind and gracious hosts.

A large tile-roofed terrace with arches surrounds the home's central area; another, with a pergola, graces the second floor and «humanizes» its scale; the guest house also has its own terrace.

All overlook the sea, and have a sense of being «honored invitees» in the otherwise-desolate landscape.

The pool, organically-shaped, faces the ocean. Its adjacent cabana offers cool shade, and cool drinks, after tennis, surfboarding and body surfing, or sunbathing.

Casa Quaccia lacks nothing; forethought, consideration and dedication make it faultless

CASA LUPTAK

A PUZZLE THAT COMES TO LIFE

LORENIA RIVA PALACIO DELMAR, ARCHITECT
DISEÑO Y CONSTRUCCIONES DYC
PROJECT

LUIS RAÚL ROMO CARRILLO, ENGINEER
DISEÑO Y CONSTRUCCIONES DYC
CONSTRUCTION

At one's initial approach, a dense garden hides the entrance, where roof tiles project above palms and eucalyptus, and architectural volume creates puzzlement: are the stairs ascending or descending?

The entranceway is perpendicular to a path, and framed by an assymetrical archway. The subtle staircase has built-in benches. Brick latticework places the home in modern Mexico, as do shiny tile floors, plaster capitals on pillars, and the ceramic roof which, surmounting both the entrance area and the house itself, provides shade inside and out.

The landscape design contrasts with the surrounding dryness: resplendent palm trees, bougainvillea in many hues, plants carrying different names and varied shades of green. From each arch, no matter how wide, there is a view of attractive foliage to gratify the spirit.

A pergola sits in the patio beside the swimming pool, with both set aginst the surrounding desert. Vines seem to tumble down into the landscape, chasing the horizon and glorifying the view.

A *talavera* border follows the swimming pool's custom contour, its blues dancing into the shimmering blue of the water, with both reflecting the blue of the sky.

The house's main area seems unattached to the earth, in its deceptive translucence. Behind it, another building attests to the home's reality — and to its beauty, with the play of terracotta tones against the garden's multitudinous greens.

Transparency and Irony

Through glass and wrought iron doors and across a floor of round flagstones, the formal entrance leads us into an otherwise informal

The house boasts of its stark simplicity to the four winds it was built to enjoy —an aggregation of spaces for refuge and for celebrating, it is a notable place for family and friends amidst desert, sea and sun.

home. First we come upon an open space under the lightly ironic roof, where we see living room, dining room and kitchen arranged in a fan-shape. This design ploy multiplies the sense of roominess without adding square meters, or unnecessary building costs; an optimal solution.

Only the economy of materials, not the care taken in locating and orienting the site within its surroundings, bespeak humility: the layout's rationale is simply comfortable living.

Stained-glass glows between the kitchen and pantry, and is reflected in windows on the exterior wall. The room is solid and light, functional and lovely.

The foliage, delightfully ornamental, also obscures and protects parts of the house. Visually and otherwise, it is boisterously playful and deeply tranquil.

A large open patio in a breathtaking landscape; witness to the dry wind chasing down from the mountains and catching the salt breeze over the ocean.

Arches seize bits of sky, ocean, desert; pillars support affable curves that gently enclose borderless terrain.

A Modicum of Privacy

At one side of the master bedrooms appears a vignette of the ocean and desert: the three bedrooms in the other direction lack even such compact views of sea and sand, but all face the central patio. The first of these bedrooms is soft, eschewing all ostentation. The bed has a view of the horizon; the terrace from this vantage has both private and public possibility. Each decorative object here is inherently, candidly, right for its setting.

Reinforced glass ensures that nothing intercede between the room and its favored location. Colors of decor are neutral, healthy and lively without drawing attention from the juxtaposition of textures and tones with earnestly useful objects.

Another bedroom serves also as a study or sitting room, with built-in bookcases and sofa-beds. It is nearest the dining room, and accessible to communal areas.

The third bedroom is more isolated, celebrating guests preferring solitude, and the privacy of the family in its comings and goings. Nearest to the entranceway and first of the three at that point, it is the last or farthest guestroom from the vantage of the communal area.

The bathrooms have views of the rear garden — windows in each look out upon the trunks of palm trees; privacy is guarded by glass brick. The bathrooms are primarily white, with decorative Mexican tiles as highlights.

Warm gatherings *al fresco*

The terrace passageway is equipped with wicker chairs, inviting residents to linger over afternoon conversations and family gatherings. Neutral tones predominate all through the

house; wood and textiles harmonizing with clay and stone.

The staircase benches are scaled for extra seating requirements, and complement the furniture.

The archway lends an air of being on a ranch almost anywhere in Mexico, whether in Sonora or Michoacan, near jungle or forest: but it is just as apt in this seaside locale.

Dining *al fresco* under the desert sun is made possible by the pergola's soft shade. It stands as a sculptural touch, too, in the simple patio and in relation to the arches beyond.

Extra Touches

Adjacent to the master bedroom, a narrow spiral staircase ascends; its tight curves giving no hint of where it actually leads. At the top, one comes upon a spectacular spot for enjoying sunsets, on the specially-designed flat roof that has itself become a showpiece.

Notable for its economy of design, the roof terrace is complete with a small garden. At one corner, a palm tree poses grandly, its canopy turned to the desert. A bench running along the entire perimeter is the only furniture necessary. Here on the terrace, confrontation with the elements, the sun behind the mountains and the salt breezes skirmishing with grains of desert sand, is controlled.

At last the sky is tinged with exotic tones as the air cools and clouds roll off to make way for the brilliant sphere's leave-taking. Ice tinkles in glasses, an occasional star ignites, the sun takes its final bows of the day.

Here from the lookout, bathed in airy hues, is surely where the sky, as it encompasses the natural world, can best be observed at any hour.

Materials declare that the house is reverently Mexican, the desert proclaims likewise. Casa Luptak displays its capabilities and revels in confounding the eye with its deceptive simplicity.

Casa Navari

Full-time family dwelling

Grupo MCA. Antonio Carrera, Architect
Project and construction

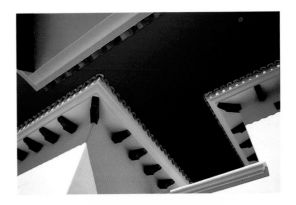

The basic idea of the house was to combine a view of the ocean with the fairway, the green. It also had to have the flavor of a hacienda, to meet the regulations of the housing development Cabo del Sol.

The inner patio serves as a vestibule, with its fountain in the center. Warm materials predominate, red marble, the rust tones of the doors, and desert plants. «We were looking something different, something original, without disregarding the established tone of the neighborhood,» says Antonio Carrera, the architect responsible for the project.

A young family from Mexico City, César, Laila and their son César, live here. They, together with Carrera, defined needs and developed solutions. The point of departure was the daily life of Laila.

César believed that «what is important in the house are the details. It from there that a house displays the care and love invested in it.»

Beach Home

This is a full-time home. The two stories are filled with spaces distributed according to conventional uses: living room, dining room, study, and guest room on the lower floor; master bedroom and a small one for their little boy on the upper floor. Each bedroom has a private bathroom and shares a terrace with a lovely view.

The kitchen is a kitchen. It is closed, typically Mexican, without that openness of kitchens in Los Cabos beach houses. The service area includes a room for domestic staff. «It is a program aligned with the daily routine of a Mexican family, not of foreigners visiting on vacation,» Carrera remarks.

It displays less spectacular characteristics than many of the constructions in the vicinity. The main attraction is its location on the golf course: opposite hole 4, which is a fairly difficult hole. The main advantage is the environment within the house, a product of close communication and accurate interpretation of needs.

Several kinds of Cuban marble cover many of the surfaces; sometimes rough, sometimes smooth, depending on its location and use. A strong, massive exterior requiring virtually no maintenance; a polished matte interior to facilitate cleaning. It is there in the windows frames, in thick pieces that seem to support the landscape outside. It covers the ends of some wooden beams of generous dimensions, so that their beauty seems contained.

It is not occupied only on short visits; its purpose is genuine domesticity. The reddish Cuban marble and the rust and ochre tones contrast with the strong color of the green and the yellow of the stone.

The rusted metal is fitting for outer doors and slides along the rising steps. Harmonious reddish and ochre tones of the marble join with the yellows of the local stone to work together as a team.

Specific Decoration

The couple themselves decided the location of the furniture, decorations, and lamps. The furnishings combine different styles with harmonious results: a heavy wooden table next to an avant guard sofa, an antique sewing machine with an ultra-modern piece of glass; antagonistic in appearance, joined by an innate aesthetic sensibility. So the decoration seems a family as well, with that insolent, playful touch of good taste, without much concern for what is orthodox.

The vestibule consists of harmonic verticality with organic lines that sinuously sway back and forth. It matches the warmth of the wood, with the coldness of stone and metal. A round arch separates the living room from the dining room. Both face the garden through sliding doors. These environments hold the decorative objects selected by the Navari with pleasure.

The ceiling of the living room, which is four meters high, has massive beams made of local palo de arco wood set at a perpendicular angle. The neighboring rooms display a lighter design, without the *palo de arco*, and with a greater closeness between the beams and the axes.

Only one room looks toward the central patio. It is the guest room and its location makes it independent from the rest of the house. «We

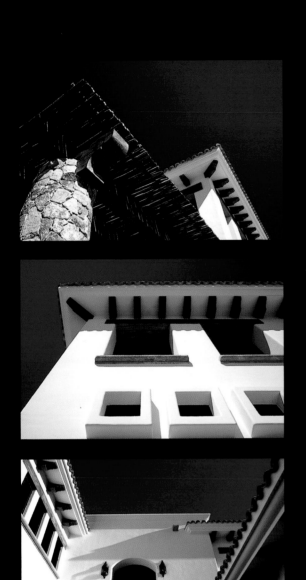

wanted to be able to continue with our daily routine, yet we wanted our guests to feel happy,» explains Laila.

Background

There are height restrictions for retaining walls: three meters facing the golf club and six meters toward the street. The character and design imposed by the required use of «Californian colonial architecture» mold the majority of houses in the Cabo del Sol housing development, Carrera says. The challenge for creative minds resides precisely in departing from the homogeneity of the model without violating the rules.

The land of Casa Navari measures 1,000 square meters with 400 square meters of construction. This provides space for the daily life of Laila and César, the toys of the toddler, and the visits of friends.

This home is the dwelling of a family who enjoys sharing the bounties of a quiet spot like Los Cabos. Its inner mission is more important than the outer scenery, although it is certainly appreciated and enjoyed.

Another Level

One ascends a stairway to the second floor, which widens out at the top. On the landing there are two doors: an old one, set in a small arch, is like a bridge to other times, other worlds, other homes. It would open to a realm that is not real, and recreates a fantasy still unimagined. It is set off by another door, which opens onto a balcony dominating the patio, the fountain, the cactus, the here and now.

The upper vestibule opens out onto a terrace roofed with palo de arco, with benches

at one of its corners, and potted flowers marking the lines of sight. The beams reappear as a border around the roof. It has a box seat for golf fans; from there, one has a great view of hole 4, and the drinks are on the house, as one waits for the dead perfect shot.

«We wanted a comfortable, functional house, that shelters both guests and us, something cozy and easy to keep up,» comments Laila. The result does not stray from the owners' wishes; the couple is fully satisfied with the results.

Palpable Achievements

Imagine that little César comes home from school, heat of the desert stuck to his uniform. He throws down his backpack, and he peels off his clothes. He runs downstairs to have a quick jump in the pool. For him, it doesn't matter that the pool is at the level of the terrace floor, without raised borders, that the grill is made of the same marble, that it has an integrated jacuzzi and is the perfect size for exercise and relaxing. The only thing that matters to him is that it is there, full of cool, fresh water, waiting for him.

Sometimes, the same little boy, playing basketball in the patio or driving one of his pedal-powered vehicles runs like a shot into the bathroom by the entrance, not noticing that the sink is a block of stone with an opening in the center. He simply assumes that this is normal, because it is part of his world. And he loves it.

*The patio functions as a vestibule,
the primary entryway that announces
without revealing. It invites you to enter,
passing the central fountain, past the rust
of the doors, and the red marble of the floor.*

Casa en la Arena

Far from the crowd

Monroy Arquitectos. Marco A. Monroy / José M. Monroy
Project and construction

Two young architects, José Miguel and Marco Monroy, were commissioned for this project. The client simply wanted a refuge, a place to get away from everyday turmoil. The result was Casa en la Arena (Dune House): a beach mansion whose interior is suited to family living, proof that wishes can surely come true.

The path leading to the house is exposed to the scorching desert sun. Nothing escapes its merciless rays; nor tempers its heat. A few palm trees in a modest verdant and flowery spot serve as decoration, but offer no shade. A row of natural poles, not quite a fence, denotes the boundary between private property and the arid immensity of the outlying landscape.

The house's message is clear: life goes on indoors and entrance is by invitation only. In a serious refuge like this, invitations are rarely extended to outsiders.

Shade within the house, however, is free and abundant. An ornamental plant stand, filled with stones and sand reminding one again of the arid surroundings, covers the roots of a tree trunk. The living and dining rooms extend into the kitchen, the areas merging in a calm unity. Heavy furniture would seem to be out of context, but curiously enough adds to the relaxed atmosphere.

Casa en la Arena is a place where the family may simply relax for awhile during frequent visits to the paradise of Baja California Sur.

In the Shadow of the Arch

«Rather than a distinct style, what we had in mind was comfort,» explains José Miguel Monroy. And he adds, «The owner wanted something very specific: high ceilings, cross ventilation, terraces, gardens, swimming pool, all skillfully interrelated.»

This interior integrity, and not a «knockout» facade, was the key design element.

Outside, what is most arresting is the house's setting, there in the very «middle of the desert.» Approximately 40 by 50 meters of land surround the 480 square meter building, constructed in early 1998. The seaside location, and the privilege of spacious isolation, add to the house's distinction.

«Life in Los Cabos, for vacationers and particularly for celebrities, means space and time to rest. They come to bask in the sun on the terrace, to walk along the beach, to be where nobody can bother them.»

The owner had a clear idea of what the house should be when he described it to the Monroys: a large swimming pool, a spacious

It's at the edge of the sea, surrounded by the beach. The mountains are distant and the house pays them no mind. It is a dwelling of decisive taste and firm conviction.

terrace for sun-bathing, a pergola that could also serve as an outdoor grill and dining room.

Outside the mansion is bold, its lack of shade reminding, «keep your distance.»

A Clear Intent

A Roman arch, 1.50 meters high, filled by a rustic door, provides entrance to the home.

In its shelter, there is some natural coolness. Still, one needs to move inside to escape the constant perspiration that forms and evaporates in this climate.

This oasis looks out upon a sparsely-ornamented entrance garden. This area, reflecting a «hands off» respect for the landscape and incorporating wild plants, might not even be construed as a garden at first glance.

At last we are inside. Our host, unsurprised, is entertained by our reaction to the the main room, which then becomes a terrace, bordered by a lawn, with its pergola and swimming pool. Upon reflection, such good-humored simplicity suggests a careful design with clear intent.

The entrance hall contrasts the antiquity of the door and ceiling beams with contemporary touches. Its most striking feature is a single tree trunk, planted in an ornamental flower stand filled with pebbles and desert sand, beside an insect sculpture by Sergio Bustamante.

The entire floor is covered with unpolished, sand-colored marble, cut cross-grain.

The desert is not completely shut out: it filters into the house in details, materials, and designs. The mansion exists in slow motion, balancing between desert and tropical heat.

The house is a single wing, with its spaces virtually all at one level. Divisions between areas are suggested by motifs in the floor, and an occasional rise indicates transition to another zone. Planned and constructed to overlook the sea, the house's side walls prohibit views of or by any future neighbors.

The reception hall, a large space designed for social gatherings, measures 4.50 meters in height: pine beams support its ceiling. It is a spacious, pleasant, enjoyable space measuring approximately five by twenty meters. Its eclectic decoration reflects the interests, and the interest in relaxing, of the people who live in the house.

The room is furnished with armchairs upholstered in tobacco brown, and carved and gilded wooden tables.

A huge oval glass-topped table with a volcanic stone base presides over the dining room with medallion-backed chairs, also covered in dark brown, arranged around it.

The kitchen, which also forms part of this area, has a kind of an inner pergola, also of pine trunks, which complements the pergola outside.

This canopy or bower is thatched with leaves from the *palo de arco*, a lightweight wood commonly used throughout the region by even the earliest builders.

The same thatch covers the surrounding wall. In desert areas, the half-shade provided by this roofing material offers the most agreeable option for staying outside, as total shade can be too cool, while full sun can be scorchingly hot.

«When we were working on the project, we did have a greater elevation in mind for the walls and ceilings, but we also wanted to keep all the structures within human proportions. We opted for a compromise: high ceilings can be quite

spectacular, but they do not give you the same feeling of coziness, of being at home.»

Enchanting Niches

Arches set the stage and are repeated in several areas: one of them captures the view in the living room, between the large sliding windows. In the dining room, an arch is cut out of the wall to accomodate a huge stucco shell, a meter in depth, which holds an assortment of tequilas and other liquor.

The Monroys work with massive forms reflecting long Mexican architectural tradition. The house's mass also gives a feeling of natural protection against extreme climactic conditions, and common-sense design for a desert mansion. The project borrowed from the glittering scenery,

assimilating spectacular views of sea and desert; but sought also to enliven the land by creating a scene of family comfort.

The result is an honest eclecticism: wrought iron, quarry stone and carved wooden sculptures, all provide counterpoint to the building's more serious side.

Step by Step

The house's refinement is in its visual effects: surprising images at the turn of a corner or the passage into another interior space.

Marble floors throughout the entire house are adorned with a distinctive stone ribbon design, which wanders to and fro as it traces the domestic geography — guiding its inhabitants and setting boundaries for its visitors.

At both ends of the corridor which leads to the family's private quarters are niches housing sculptures by famous craftsmen. The first room off the corridor looks over the sea, then its view stretches into the desert, seeming to forget that it is part of a beach mansion.

Here the interior becomes a space with no other pretensions than to shelter the family. Bathrooms, bedrooms, interior courtyards surprise by their everyday quality; they'd look at home in a domestic setting anywhere. But the windows remind us of the desert: typically small, they keep out strong sunlight and heat.

The bathrooms are simple: decorated with *talavera*, they have tile floors and marble counters. Dome skylights admit natural light.

Decorations simply create a sense of tranquility amidst daily life. Simplicity triumphs, as materials transcend their original forms: branches join to become a fence, a roof, shelter and coolness.

The master bedroom also has small windows, which yet present residents with views of the famous Cabos. Furniture suggests Mayan design. As in the rest of the house, niches add interest to the walls. The adjoining bathroom is more spacious, more definite in its style, than one might have expected.

But the master suite's most splendid feature is its rooftop terrace, with its canopy of palm leaves and magnificent view. To reach it, stairs spiral to a height of 3.5 meters. Upholstered divans complete the terrace's decor.

The sea is important, but less important than the family activities which go on within the walls of the house, within sight of the ocean.

Myriad Sense Impressions

Apart from its spatial fascination and views, the mansion evokes myriad sense impressions. It is a haven in the middle of the desert; the sea its sole companion. With no neighbors nor development around, and the mountains standing guard in the background, it is a privileged refuge for the owners and their very closest friends.

And along with its formal statements, the house is designed to function usefully, without fanfare, for its inhabitants. It honors the landscape within which it is set, and at the same time it humbly enriches that landscape with scenes from its family milieu. This is a luxurious but discriminating mansion, with incomparable places like the rooftop terrace for viewing the spectacular sunsets and starry nights that only desert zones can produce.

CASA ÉTNICA

A VILLA WITH A TOUCH OF MUSEUM

MITCH PARR
DIRECTOR, HOTEL CABO SAN LUCAS

KATHERINE NIDERMAIER
PROJECT AND DECORATION

They are villas with different dimensions. With seven, five or three bedrooms. They accomodate guests from the Hotel Cabo San Lucas, and each one is adorned with ethnic Mexican artesanry. They offer almost formal lessons in the cultures of different indigenous groups, respectful teachings of their heritage, a tribute to the arts of people still devoted to nature as a universal Mother.

The structure itself is lost among the palms, the road that leads to it barely announces its existence. From a distance one sees only the red roofs among the green. From the beach, one sees its terraces, open to the sea; some along the murmuring sands, others above the steep rocks and crashing waves.

«The project tries to rescue the Mexico of Mexico; to show the tourist that indigenous art is not only in the Museum of Anthropology or in books and magazines, but that indigenous art of Mexico is alive,» says the U.S. designer, Katherine Nidermaier.

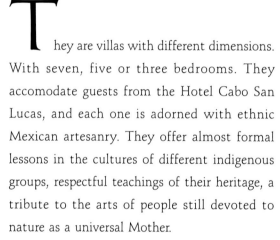

To complete the project took four years. «First I did research: in books, professional journals, the Internet. Then followed the selection of ethnic groups for the different themes of the villas. To make the selection, we had to come up with sufficient atesanry to fill various rooms. We had to speak directly with the artesans, in their own dialects. Romanticism? Perhaps. There is a certain magic in speaking to the past.»

Katy speaks of her fears that the works would not be appreciated, or respected. «We placed literature about the culture and its art in each villa with the idea of helping the guest understand, and learn.»

Filigreed Huipil

The Villa Maya welcomes its guests with ten clay ocelots, decorated in red, lined up under a window. The roof is covered with straw, it's two stories high, held aloft by a large beam across the apex. There are five habitations, aligned in

Here are four formal lessons, concerning four indigenous Mexican cultures. They are respectful, and well documented. It is an attempt to recapture, and to raise autochthonous artesanry to the level of art. It is a response to the contact with people who still speak their native languages and communicate with their ancestors in their continuous search for knowledge.

opposing directions, joined by a central module with living room, dining room, kitchen and service area.

Each space takes its neighbor into consideration; they share amicably, but keep a respectful distance. The terrace is a semi-circle looking over the sea. It has a stone floor and dark wood furniture. There are doors to the bedrooms, and a common corridor and small gardens here and there.

The main sitting room is illuminated by two enormous lamps of beaten tin and beveled glass. The furnishings are of textiles in natural colors: a covered armchair, a quarry stone table, a book on Mayan Culture. Above the fireplace there is a painting of an ocelot in the form of a man, or man in the form of ocelot.

Blue predominates in the picture, as it predominates in the textiles that adorn the villa. From intense cobalt, to pale sky blue embroidery.

Mexican ethnic groups speak their word in these villas; accompanied by an ocean beach that does not contrast with the formality of their aesthetic proposals, nor does it lessen the mastery of the their artesanry.

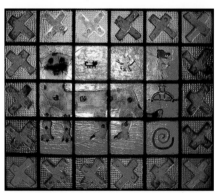

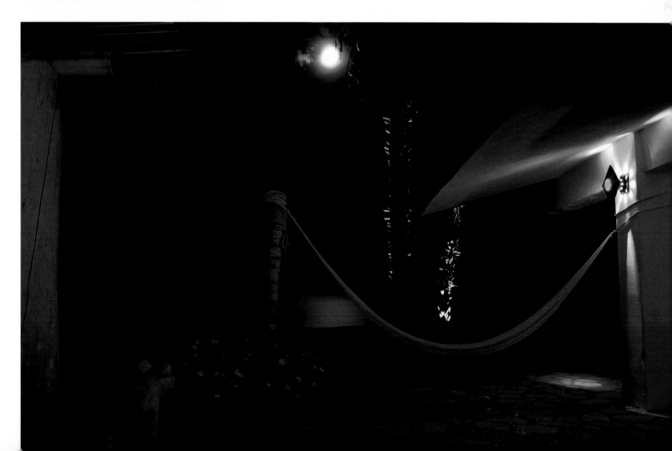

On Site Lessons

At the entrance to Villa Maya, the first huipil adorns the vestibule. It is by María López, from San Andrés Larráisar; it's behind acrylic and has an information card attached. It has been worked masterfully in colors of blue and pink. The dining room boasts a floor of circular stone. The table is made of four sections of marble. A fishing basket has been converted into a lamp and difuse light casts playful shadows throughout the room. On one wall, a sun is reflected in a mirror whose frame is polished wood. There is a suspended ledge which holds various pieces of artesanry and basketry.

One bedroom of the central building is particularly priveleged. One comes to it after encountering a stained glass of blues and yellows, and finds the bedroom decorated in beige, which sets off the collection of embroidered bedspreads, and a white huipil on the wall.

The other habitations repeat the basic elements. Color tones are different from room to room, some blue, others are various combinations of blues and reds. It's the textiles that make the difference.

Pictures in Thread

A wide door, beneath a large beam and divided by a strong column, opens onto transparency via a network of glass. In front, a fountain on floor level and covered in round rock hides its true function. It's called Villa Pátzcuaro.

The sitting room seems full of rubicund color, festive shapes and bedspreads of bucolic scenery. The green clay pine cones are placed in niches in the walls, the blue tiles of the kitchen are handpainted. A painting dominates the space, an angel absorbed in the heart it carries in

its hands. A pair of rebosos are hung on walls, each from poles of worked wood. The dining room is of finished wood, painted with crowned cherubim as back rests; the comode has flowers, and the ample credenza speaks of forceful chisel work.

The seven bedrooms are like sitting rooms in museums: with special areas to view the white embroidered dress, winner of the National Artesanry Prize of 1997, to give but one example. Details are repeated without tiring the eye, objects surprise us not only by their craft, but by their placement: door handles in the form of snails and shells, bows and arrows in the bathroom, medals in lampstands, hats adorning the bedstead, photographs of Indians in antique frames one would use for grandparents.

Villas Tarahumara and Mitla

The figures and materials of these habitations warn immediately of a culture from unknown lands; it appears a little out of place in Los Cabos, a land of desert and sea. But it does not matter

that the murmur of the sea is nearby, that the sun shines brilliantly, that the beach is near to hand. What matters is the respect for the culture that pervades this place: wooden horses, simple and haughty; a human couple carved partly in wood, partly in stone; woolens and leather worked pillows. Force and rigor in everything, with waves crashing into rocks as background music.

The construction is basically the same in all the villas, but this one is more ample in its roofs and is gathered together in less space. There are three bedrooms which keep to the tarahumara motif in textiles, adornments, sculptures, baskets, wrought iron.

The Villa Mitla receives the visitor with a panel of worked quarry stone as an outer wall, accompanied by a mermaid. Tiled floors, stones set even in the kitchen counter, fantastic figures carved in brightly painted wood, stone filigree over the fireplace. Mermaids abound, as well as beaten tinwork and baskets. The star of this enclosure is a dress from Gelaguetza, Oaxaca.

Green clay pine cones from Michoacan, Maya huipiles, ceremonial dresses from Oaxaca. These precious and valuable works are on display not only as adornment but as part of an effort to share a profound and distant art.

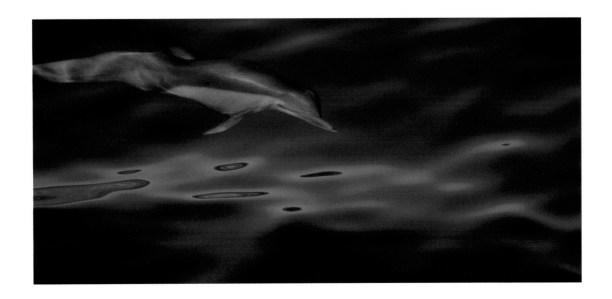

*Our special thanks
to the following people for the collaboration
which made this book possible:*

*Ing. Miguel Ángel Arce
Arq. Jacinto Avalos
Arq. Birl Binkley
Arq. Douglas Burdge
Arq. Luis Cano
Arq. Antonio Carrera
Ing. Jorge Carrera
Sr. Mark Ehremberg
Sra. Tracy Ehremberg
Sr. Fernando Estrada
Sr. Carlos González Ceseña
Ing. Elías Gutiérrez Osuna
Sr. Julio López
Arq. Marco A. Monroy
Arq. José M. Monroy
Katherine Nidermaier
Sr. Mitch Parr
Arq. Lorenia Riva Palacio
Sr. Ricardo Rode
Ing. Luis Raúl Romo Carrillo
Arq. Próspero Tapia
Sra. Federica Wilkins*

Houses of Los Cabos was printed in December, 1999, in Hong Kong, coodinated by Global Interprint, Inc. It was designed with Page Maker 6.5 and Corel Draw 8. It is set in Carleton and Schneidler fonts. Printed on 150 gm. couché gloss paper, in 5x5 colors and varnish. The production of the book was supervised by Ángeles Fahara, Miriam Reyes and Mauricio Martínez. 180 pages with dustcover.